W9-AIU-824

⊕ Rand McNally
STUDENT'S WORLD ATLAS

Rand McNally
STUDENT'S WORLD ATLAS

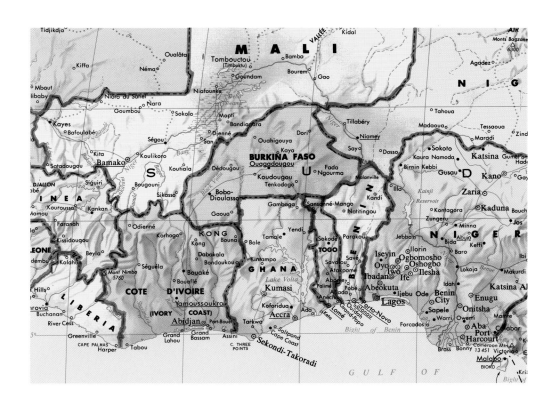

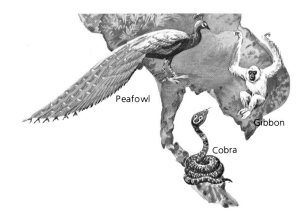

Peafowl

Gibbon

Cobra

Rand McNally Student's World Atlas

General manager: Russell L. Voisin
Managing editor: Jon M. Leverenz
Editor: Elizabeth Fagan Adelman
Production editor: Laura C. Schmidt
Manufacturing planner: Marianne Abraham

Rand McNally Student's World Atlas
Copyright © 1994 by Rand McNally & Company
Revised Printing 1998

Photograph Credits
Pages 4-5: Pakistan/Ric Ergenbright; Alps/Rand McNally Pictorial World Atlas. **8-9:** Earth/NASA 72-HC-928; Mt. St. Helens/R. Hoblitt/United States Geological Survey; San Andreas Fault/R.E. Wallace/United States Geological Survey. **10-11 :** Hurricane Elena/NASA; Lightning/Francis Reddy. **12-13:** Plankton bloom/Dennis Clark; North America/U.S. Air Force Defense Meteorological Satellite Program. **14-15:** Moonrise/NASA; Moon/NASA 88-H-372; Impact/ ©William Hartmann/ All rights reserved. **22-23:** Alps/Rand McNally Pictorial World Atlas; County Kerry/Ric Ergenbright; Mykonos/Rand McNally Student's World Atlas. **29:** Eiffel Tower/Joe Viesti. **34:** China and Pakistan/Ric Ergenbright. **40:** Jerusalem/Rand McNally Pictorial World Atlas, Colour Library International Limited. **44-45:** Zambia/Rand McNally Atlas of Mankind; Gulf of Guinea/Anna Tully, Hutchinson Picture Library. **50-51:** Masai/Rand McNally Children's World Atlas; Tunisia/R.G. Williamson, Telegraph Colour Library; Zimbabwe/Christopher Arnesen, Allstock. **56-57:** Australia/Robert Ivey, Ric Ergenbright Photography; New Caledonia/Christopher Arnesen, Allstock. **64-65:** Caribbean/Nathan Benn, Allstock; Monument Valley and British Columbia/Ric Ergenbright. **70-71:** Mexico City/Rand McNally Pictorial World Atlas; Washington D.C./Art Wolfe, Allstock. **78-79:** Peru/Ric Ergenbright; Guyana/Hutchinson Picture Library; Paraguay/Peter Keen, Telegraph Colour Library. **84-85:** Suriname/R. Phillips, Image Bank; Rio de Janerio (cover photo) Robert Ivey, Ric Ergenbright Photography; Ecuador/Rand McNally Pictorial World Atlas. **89:** Antarctica/Rand McNally Pictorial World Atlas.

Every effort has been made to trace the copyright holders of the photographs in this publication. Rand McNally apologizes in advance for any unintentional omissions and would be pleased to insert the appropriate acknowledgment in any subsequent edition of this book.

Library of Congress Cataloging-in-Publication Data

Rand McNally and Company.
    Student's world atlas. -- Rev. [ed.]
        p.   cm.
    Includes index.
    ISBN 0-528-83699-4
    1. Children's Atlases. [1. Atlases.] I. Title.
G1021.R47   1994   <G&M>
912--dc20   93-41312
                                   CIP
                                 MAP AC

Contents

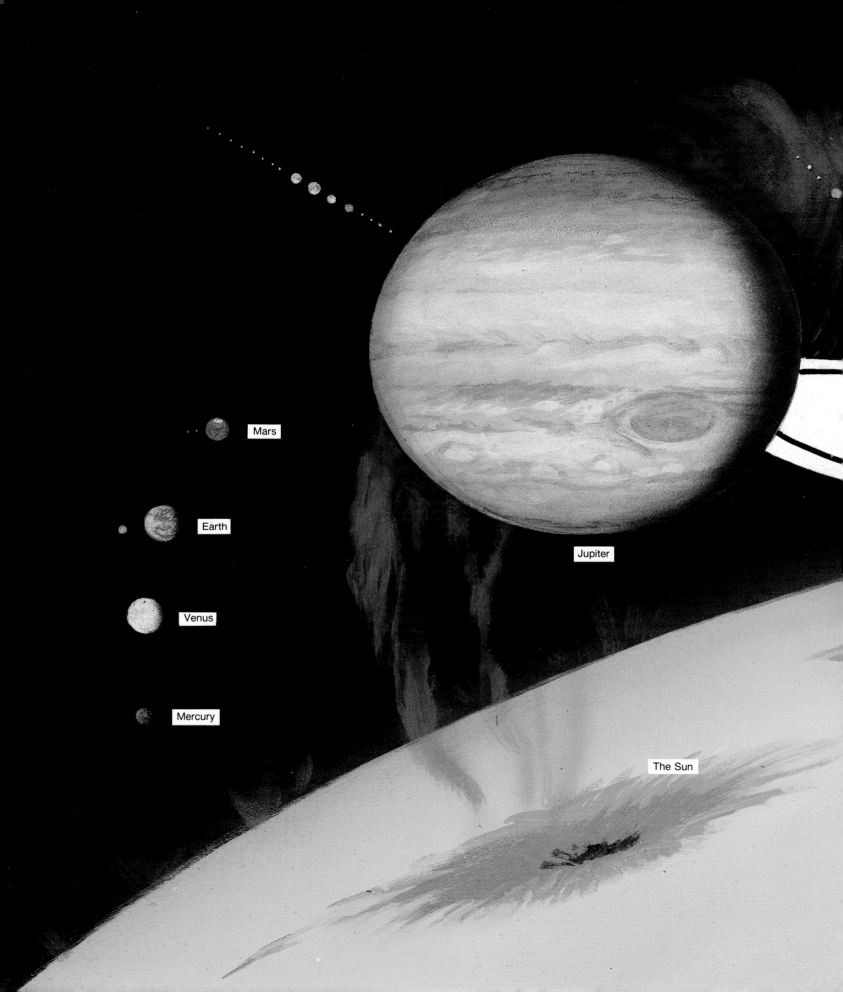

Mars

Earth

Venus

Mercury

Jupiter

The Sun

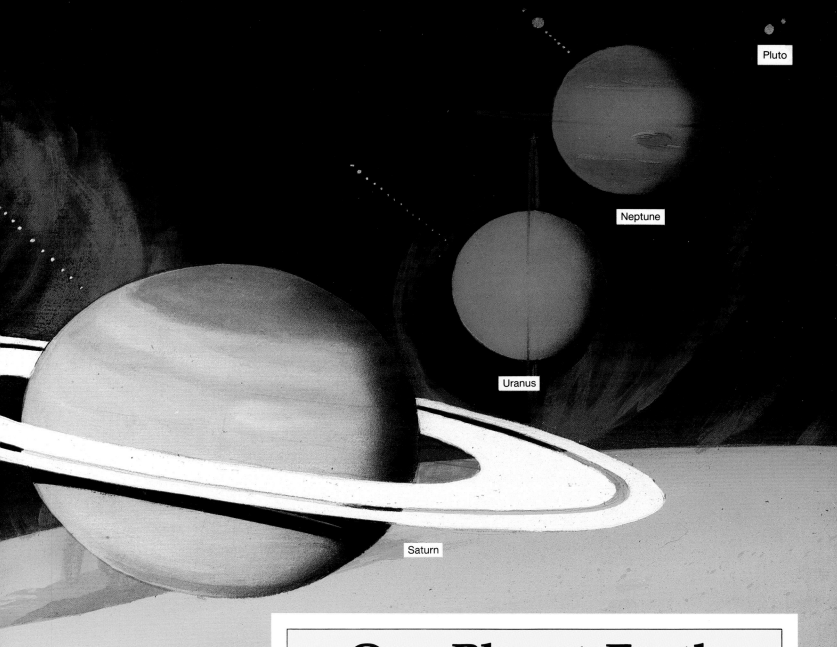

Pluto

Neptune

Uranus

Saturn

Our Planet Earth
The Solar System:
The Earth's Neighborhood

This portrait of the solar system shows all nine planets and sixty moons at the same scale. The sun, represented by the flaming arc at the bottom, is too large to fit into the picture. The planet earth is dwarfed in size by the giant planets of the outer solar system.

OUR PLANET EARTH
A World of Rock

When one plate slides under another, molten rock works its way upward. A fresh source of molten rock reactivated Mount St. Helens in Washington State.

The movement of the North American and Pacific crustal plates splits a stream that crosses their boundary—California's San Andreas fault.

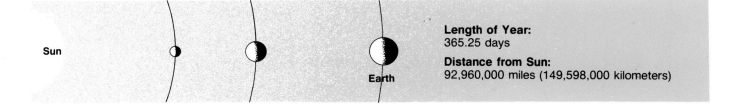

Sun

Earth

Length of Year:
365.25 days

Distance from Sun:
92,960,000 miles (149,598,000 kilometers)

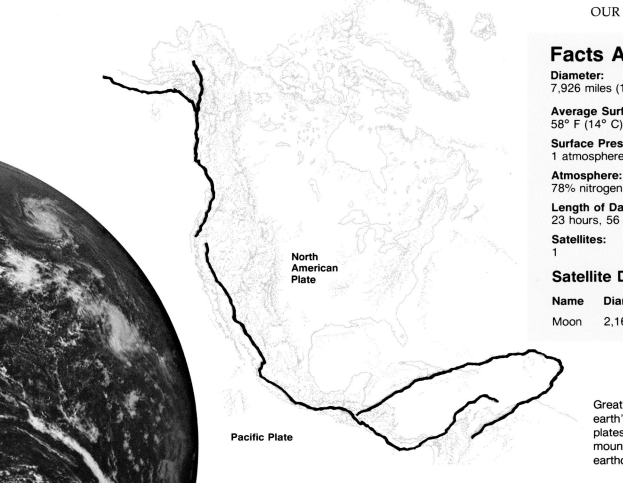

North American Plate

Pacific Plate

Facts About Earth

Diameter:
7,926 miles (12,756 km)

Average Surface Temperature:
58° F (14° C)

Surface Pressure:
1 atmosphere

Atmosphere:
78% nitrogen, 21% oxygen

Length of Day:
23 hours, 56 minutes

Satellites:
1

Satellite Data

Name	Diameter
Moon	2,160 miles (3,476 km)

Great fractures break the earth's crust into huge rocky plates. Their motions build mountains and create earthquakes and volcanoes.

Earth's clouds swirl above the familiar outline of Africa (top left to center) and mix with the icy glare of Antarctica's polar cap (bottom right). Our home, the earth, is a truly special—and fragile—planet.

E arth is a very special planet. It shares the solar system with eight other worlds, each with its own unique characteristics. Studying these alien landscapes makes the familiar features of earth seem even more special. In the next few pages we'll study the earth as a planet and explore its place in the solar system.

Unlike any other planet, earth's surface constantly changes. The crust is cracked into a dozen separate fragments called *tectonic plates* that float on a sea of dense, semi-liquid rock. Temperatures rise underneath the crust, and where they exceed 1,700° F (900° C), the rock turns into a thick liquid. Columns of this molten rock slowly rise and fall within the earth, nudging the crustal plates that float on the surface. As the plates try to move, they push into their neighbors.

Earthquakes occur when the rock of two plates, locked together by pressure, suddenly fractures and allows the plates to slip. Volcanoes rumble to life when molten rock from the earth's depths finds its way to the surface. The world's great mountain ranges were formed from rock crumpled and lifted when plates smashed together in million-year-long collisions. Other planets have their own spectacles, but only earth has a surface where rock itself seems so alive.

OUR PLANET EARTH
A World of Air

The hazards of space are never far from us. Chunks of rock large and small plunge toward our planet each day. Even the sun threatens life on earth with harmful ultraviolet light and streams of dangerous particles.

A thin shell of gas called the *atmosphere* protects us from these dangers. It is made up mostly of nitrogen (78 percent) and oxygen (21 percent). If earth were reduced to the size of an apple, this protective layer of gas would be as thin as the apple's skin.

Space debris comes in two forms, natural and human-made, but both usually burn up in the atmosphere. Only

A collar of tall thunderclouds marks the central eye of Hurricane Elena, which roamed the Atlantic Ocean in 1985. Hurricanes are the most powerful storms on the planet. Spiral clouds trace air streaming into the storm center, where winds often reach speeds of over 110 miles (176 kilometers) per hour.

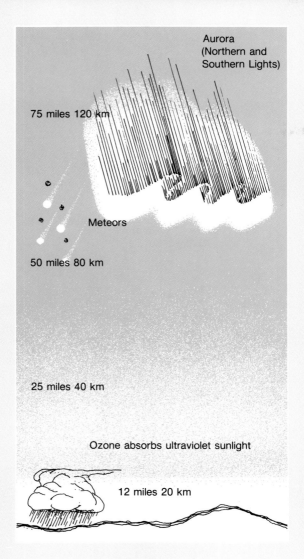

Aurora (Northern and Southern Lights)

75 miles 120 km

Meteors

50 miles 80 km

25 miles 40 km

Ozone absorbs ultraviolet sunlight

12 miles 20 km

The earth's atmosphere protects people from many dangers. Space debris as small as dust and as large as automobiles break up in the atmosphere and are often visible as shooting stars, or meteors, at night. Particles from the sun create colorful auroras when they strike air molecules, and dangerous ultraviolet sunlight is absorbed by the ozone layer. All the weather on earth occurs at the bottom of this vast ocean of air.

the largest pieces of space debris survive this fiery passage—and two-thirds of those fall into the sea.

The atmosphere also stops hazardous particles from the sun and prevents them from harming the earth and its life. Occasionally, regions of the sun flare up and blast streams of electrons and protons into space. The atmosphere absorbs the particles before they come too close to the earth's surface.

Another protective region hovers closer to the ground. Between altitudes of about ten to thirty miles (fifteen and fifty kilometers), a gas called *ozone* screens out most of the sun's harmful ultraviolet light. Mounting evidence suggests that human activity may be harming this important *ozone layer*.

Humans live at the bottom of earth's ocean of air. All of the activity we call *weather* occurs here. Water vapor keeps this part of the atmosphere constantly churning with ever-changing clouds and mighty storms that bring summer rains and winter snow. Clouds form as water vapor rises, cools, and condenses into droplets.

Of the planets in our solar system, only earth has an atmosphere rich in the oxygen we need to breathe. And this atmosphere creates an environment in which liquid water flows freely on earth's surface. This happens nowhere else in the solar system.

Lightning splits the sky during a severe thunderstorm in Milwaukee, Wisconsin. Lightning's spark breaks down nitrogen gas in the air, making chemicals that plants need to grow.

The smallest living things change the face of the planet. A satellite camera captures the bloom of microscopic marine plants in the waters off Mexico and South America. The greatest amount of plant life appears red, the lowest amount is deep blue.

A World of Life

Earth is truly the living planet. Life, in all its many forms, is our planet's most important and unique feature. According to the best counts, we share the earth with about one million different kinds of animals—most of them insects—and more than 350,000 types of plants.

Living creatures helped make earth the haven it now is. Most scientists believe that earth's atmosphere started changing billions of years ago, when marine plants with the ability to make their own food first appeared. These plants contained a green pigment called *chlorophyll*—the only substance in nature able to trap and store the energy in sunlight.

Through the process of *photosynthesis*, green plants use sunlight, water, and carbon dioxide gas to make sugar. They also give off water and oxygen gas, which shape the atmosphere we breathe today.

Life on earth is incredibly abundant. It is found almost everywhere, from the depths of the ocean floor to the peaks of the highest mountains. Even inhospitable regions teem with life. Scientists have found bacteria beneath the ice of lakes in Antarctica, which is probably earth's harshest environment.

The diversity of earth's life is also impressive. From pigeons to porpoises, life has taken on every environment

This nighttime photograph of the United States reveals a constellation of city lights. Even from space, the planet easily shows the marks of human activity.

available—land, sea, and air. Scientists rush to discover and classify the plants, insects, and animals of the great tropical rain forests that girdle the earth's equatorial regions. These areas are threatened with destruction as human inhabitants clear the forests in an effort to create farmland.

When astronauts look down on earth from a spaceship, they do not need special equipment to find signs of life. Many signs of human activity stand out from space. For example, the lush green valley of Africa's Nile River traces a dark line through the light-colored sands of the Sahara Desert. Or perhaps the colored patterns of agriculture show up over America's Midwest, where rectangular green patches indicate grazing land and tan areas show where farmers grow wheat.

Although astronauts can see these things from their vantage point in orbit, they must look carefully to find them. A more obvious sign of human life awaits them on the night side of earth. As the sun sets on the spaceship, and a green curtain of aurora dances below at the fringes of space, the darkened earth seems to fill with stars. Beneath, where millions of people fight off the darkness, the twinkling glow of city lights reveals a coastline. Only lightning from a thunderstorm challenges these human-made constellations.

The moon's familiar face rises above a cloudy earth. It is earth's nearest neighbor in space, circling the planet once each month. The only celestial body on which humans have landed, the moon has become a stepping stone into the solar system.

The Moon: Our Neighbor in Space

The moon is earth's partner in a never-ending dance through space. About 2,160 miles (3,476 kilometers) across, the moon is an airless, waterless world just one-fourth the size of the earth. It circles the earth once every 27.32 days at an average distance of about 238,000 miles (384,000 km).

Only one side of the moon is visible from earth. The pull of our planet's gravity slowed the moon's spin until it exactly matched the twenty-seven-day orbital period. Now the moon completes one rotation in exactly the same time it takes to circle the earth.

As the moon slides along in its orbit, it rises into the sky an average of fifty minutes later each day. The sunlit portion of the moon's surface—the part we can see—changes daily in a cycle called the moon's *phases*.

Although the sun is four hundred times larger than the moon, it's also four hundred times farther away. Both bodies appear to be nearly the same size from earth. About once every eighteen months on average, a new moon passes directly across the face of the sun and plunges some region on earth into midday darkness—a *total solar eclipse*. Less impressive *partial eclipses*, in which the moon covers only part of the sun, occur on average every five months.

Marked by ancient lava-filled basins and giant impact craters, the moon's surface has changed very little since it formed.

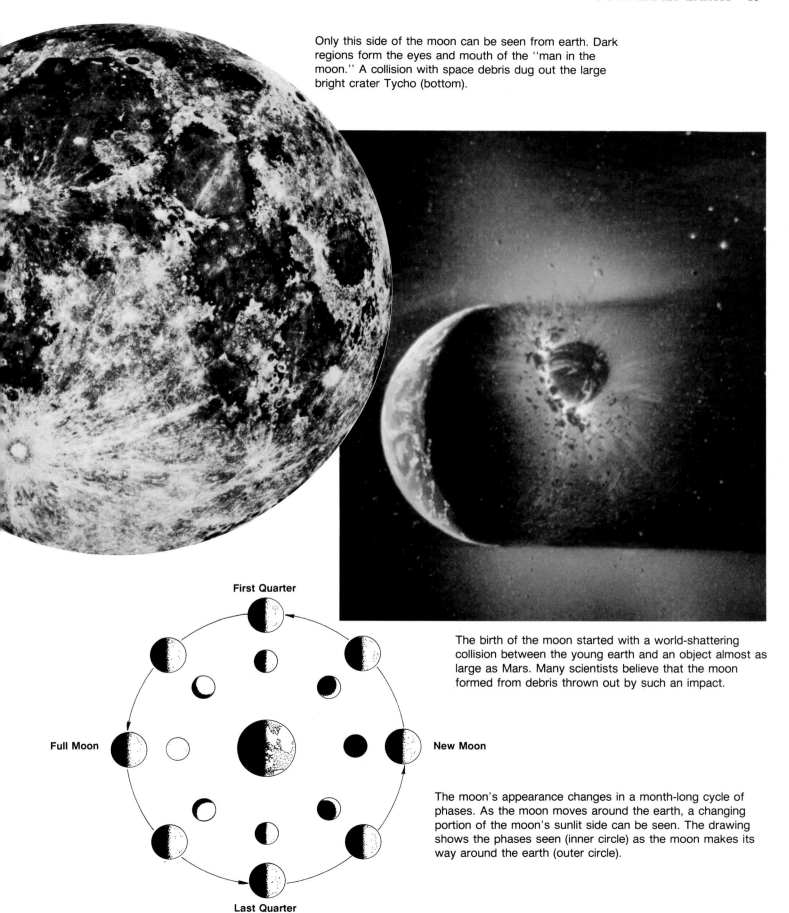

Only this side of the moon can be seen from earth. Dark regions form the eyes and mouth of the "man in the moon." A collision with space debris dug out the large bright crater Tycho (bottom).

The birth of the moon started with a world-shattering collision between the young earth and an object almost as large as Mars. Many scientists believe that the moon formed from debris thrown out by such an impact.

First Quarter

Full Moon

New Moon

Last Quarter

The moon's appearance changes in a month-long cycle of phases. As the moon moves around the earth, a changing portion of the moon's sunlit side can be seen. The drawing shows the phases seen (inner circle) as the moon makes its way around the earth (outer circle).

OUR PLANET EARTH
A World of Nations

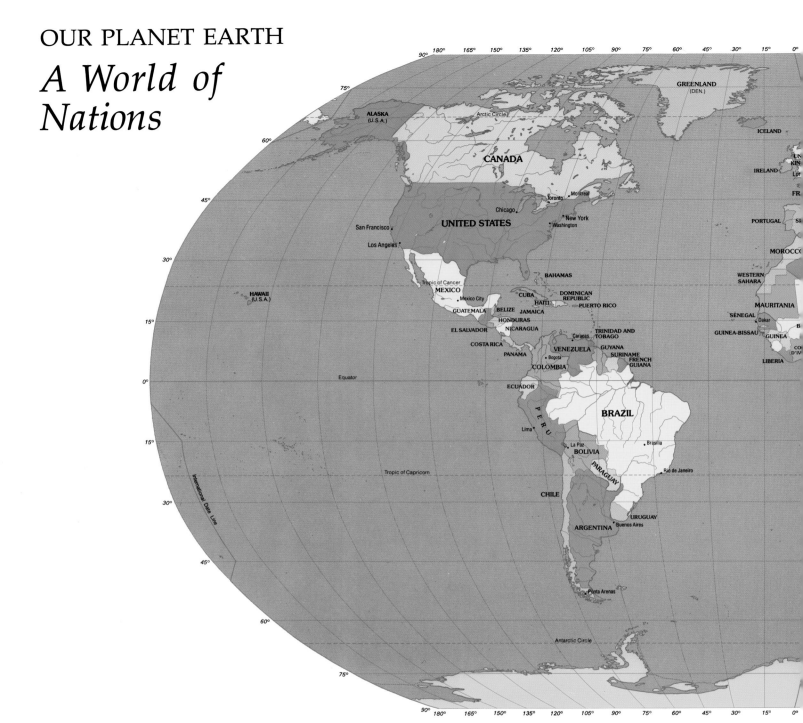

This map shows the countries of the earth. The colors simply make it easier to see each separate country on the map; they do not tell you anything about each nation. This type of map is called *political* because it shows the world's political divisions.

National borders are represented on the map as thin red lines. These lines divide the world into separate countries. Sometimes they follow natural formations such as mountain ranges or rivers. For example, the crooked northwestern border of China runs along a river. In some cases, though, the line is designated by humans—as with the straight portion of the border between Canada and the United States.

Although most political borders in today's world are well established, changes still occur. In 1990, for instance, East and West Germany united, and Germany became a single nation. In 1991, the Soviet Union dissolved, and many nations that had been a part of the union became independent.

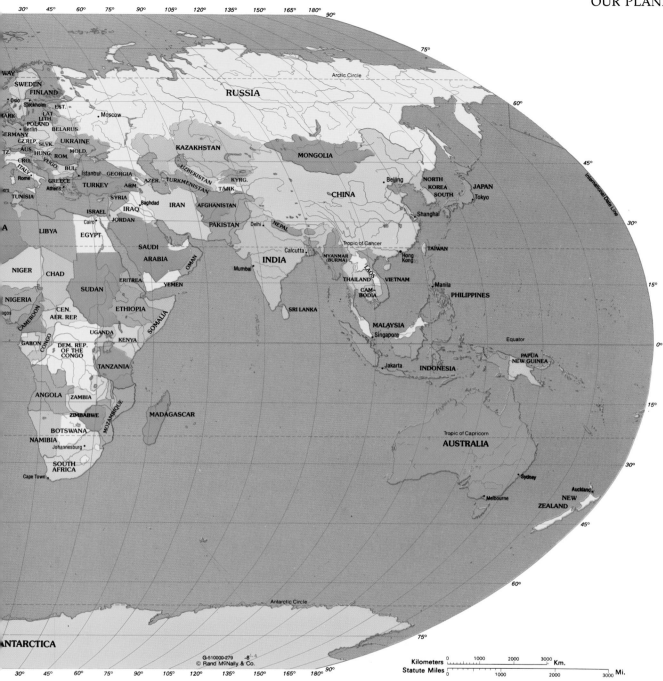

Some countries are large, and some countries are small. Russia and Canada are huge nations. The world's smallest independent state is Vatican City, in Rome, Italy.

When people study the world, they often organize all the countries by land areas called *continents*. The seven continents are the great divisions of the earth. Nearly all of them are large pieces of land that are almost completely surrounded by water.

This atlas divides the world into the seven continents: Europe, Asia, Africa, North America, South America, Antarctica, and the area in the South Pacific called Oceania. The islands of the South Pacific are grouped with Australia to form Oceania, but they are not actually part of Australia.

For each continent except Antarctica, there is a section on its *terrain*, or land areas; a discussion of its wild animals; a section about what the people who live there do for a living; and an overview of its countries and cities.

Using the Atlas

An atlas is a guide to the world that can be used in many ways. But to discover the world with your atlas, you must be able to do five things:

- Measure distances using a map scale.
- Use directions and latitude and longitude.
- Find places on the maps using map keys.
- Use different kinds of maps.
- Use map symbols and legends.

The following sections can help you learn how to do these things.

Figure 1

Measuring Distances

To understand a map, you must know its *scale*, or how large an area of the earth it shows. There are different types of map scales, but the *bar scale* is the easiest to use for finding distance.

For example, to find the distance between Bergen and Oslo in Norway, first you will find out how far Bergen is from Oslo on the map. Then, by using a bar scale, you will learn what this means in actual distance on the earth.

1. Find Bergen and Oslo on the map in Figure 1.
2. Lay a slip of paper on the map so its edge touches the two cities. Move the paper so one corner touches Bergen.
3. Mark the paper where it touches Oslo. The distance from the corner of the paper to the mark shows how far Oslo is from Bergen on the map.
4. The numbers in the map scale in Figure 2 show *statute miles*, or miles on

the earth. Line up the edge of the paper along the map scale, putting the corner at 0.

5. Find the mark on the paper. The mark shows that Bergen is about two hundred miles away from Oslo.

Using Directions and Latitude and Longitude

Most of the maps in this atlas are drawn so north is at the top of the page, south is at the bottom, west is at the left, and east is at the right.

Many of the maps also have lines drawn across them—lines of *latitude* and *longitude*. These are lines drawn on a map or globe to make it easier to tell directions and to locate places.

Latitude lines are also called *parallels*. As shown in Figure 3, lines of latitude run east and west. The equator is a line of latitude, and it runs around the middle of the earth. Other lines of latitude measure how far north or south of the equator a place is. Lines of latitude are numbered in *degrees*,

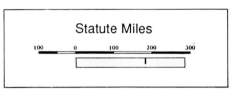

Figure 2

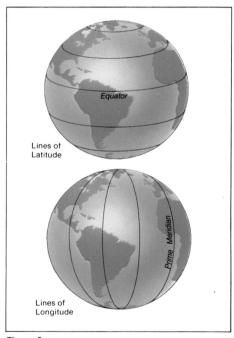

Figure 3

which measure the distance.

The equator is at zero degrees (0°) latitude. The numbers go up in each direction (north and south) the farther you get from the equator. The map in Figure 1 shows that Bergen is north of sixty degrees (60°) latitude and

Stockholm is south of it. So Bergen is farther north than Stockholm.

Lines of longitude run north and south between the two poles, as you can see from Figure 3. Longitude lines are also called *meridians*. Like latitude, longitude is also measured in degrees.

The *prime meridian* is at zero degrees (0°) longitude. Lines of longitude measure how far east or west a place is from the prime meridian. The numbers go up as you travel in each direction (east and west). In Figure 1, Bergen is about five degrees (5°) east of the prime meridian, and Stockholm is about twenty degrees (20°) east. So Stockholm is farther east than Bergen.

Using Map Keys

One of the most important things an atlas can do is tell you the location of a place. To help you find a place quickly and easily on a map, most atlases have an index that includes both the names of places and a guide that is made up of a letter and a number, or a *map key*.

Say you want to find Santiago, a city in Chile, which is in South America. Here's how you would use the map key.

1. Look up the city's name, Santiago, in the back of the atlas. You'll see an entry like the one in Figure 4. The number *88* is the page on which the map is found. The map key *C2* is the letter-number guide to finding Santiago on the map on page 88.
2. Look at Figure 5. It is a piece of the map of southern South America that you will find on page 88.
3. Find the letters *A* through *C* along the left-hand side of the map. Then find the numbers *2* through *4* along the top edge of the map. These numbers and letters are centered between the lines of latitude and longitude on the map.
4. To find Santiago, use the map key *C2*. Place your left index finger on *C* and your right index finger on *2*. Move your left finger across the map and your right finger down the map, staying within the

Figure 4

Figure 5

88 South America, South • Physical — Political

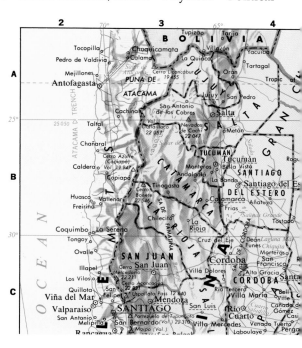

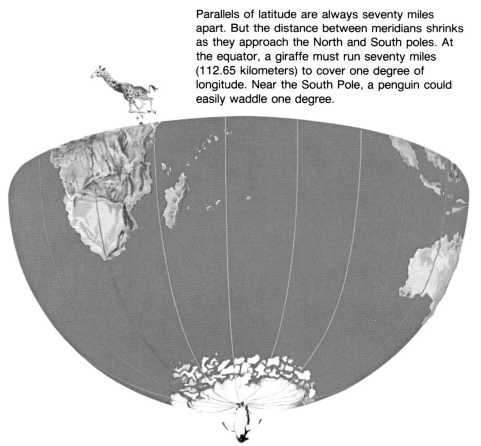

Parallels of latitude are always seventy miles apart. But the distance between meridians shrinks as they approach the North and South poles. At the equator, a giraffe must run seventy miles (112.65 kilometers) to cover one degree of longitude. Near the South Pole, a penguin could easily waddle one degree.

USING THE ATLAS

latitude and longitude lines on either side. Your fingers will meet in the box that contains Santiago.

You can use this method to find any place listed in the index of this atlas. If you see a small, or lowercase, letter in a map key, it refers to the small inset map on the page rather than to the main map on the page. Two map keys are shown for areas that begin on one map and continue on another map.

Using Different Kinds of Maps

There are many different types of maps, and each is especially suited for a certain purpose. For exploring the world's surface, *terrain maps* reveal rugged mountains and continental plains. For special subjects, such as the wildlife of a region, *thematic* maps provide an easy way to see differences throughout the world. For studying countries, *political maps* display the world's nations and cities, roads, and railways. The *physical-political* maps in this atlas tell you the most about each continent. They are the large maps on the pages all by themselves.

The terrain maps go along with the section on the terrain of each continent. These are also called *physical maps* because they show only the physical features of the land. Physical features include oceans, lakes, rivers, glaciers, mountains, and other natural parts of the world.

The thematic maps go with the sections on animals and life on the land. The thematic maps show pictures that tell you about different regions on the map. On the thematic map of the animals of North America, you can see that raccoons live around the Great Lakes. Similar maps throughout the atlas show the kinds of

Terrain Map

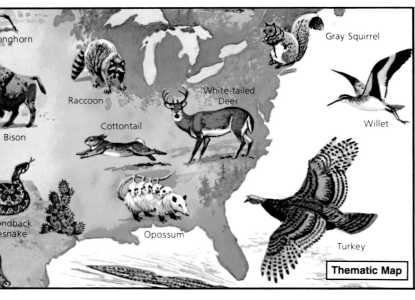

Thematic Map

Political Map

© 1979 Rand McNa

Physical-political Map

wildlife found on each continent. Another type of thematic map shows how people use the land of each continent.

The political maps show the world's political units, the human-made divisions of the earth's surface into countries, states, and cities. These maps go with the sections about countries and cities. They show you the boundaries of each country on the continent as well as the major cities. On the political map of North America, for instance, thick gray lines represent the boundaries of countries. Thinner gray lines show the borders between states or provinces. The thinnest gray lines reveal the locations of railroad tracks; red lines show the major roadways. Other countries, such as Canada and Mexico, are shaded with different colors.

When people think about maps, they usually picture physical-political maps. To get the most information out of these maps, you need to understand what the special symbols on each map represent. You can do that with the help of a *legend*, which is discussed in the next section.

Using Map Symbols and Legends

The easiest way to describe a *symbol* is that it is something that stands for something else. In a way, a whole map is a symbol, because it represents the world or a part of it.

The world's features—such as cities, rivers, and lakes—are represented with symbols on maps. The legend tells you what these symbols mean. On the physical-political maps in this atlas, the symbol for a city might be a dot or a red shaded area, depending on how big the city is. Rivers are shown with blue lines, and railroads are indicated with red lines.

The physical-political map legend at the right divides the earth's geographic features into three major classes: cultural, land, and water features. Cultural features are human-made and include cities, railroads, dams, and political boundaries. Land features are mountain peaks, mountain passes, and *spot heights*. Spot heights tell you the elevation of certain places on a mountain. Water features include rivers, lakes, swamps, and glaciers. Refer to this when working with the physical-political maps.

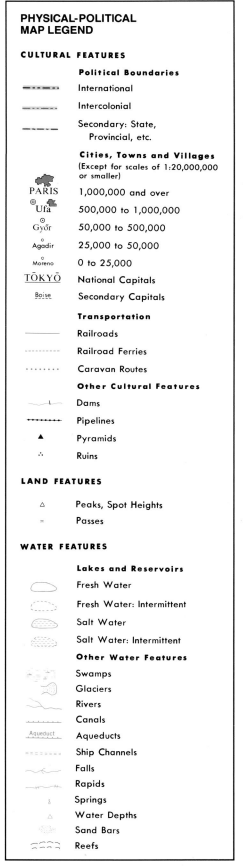

PHYSICAL-POLITICAL MAP LEGEND

CULTURAL FEATURES

Political Boundaries

International

Intercolonial

Secondary: State, Provincial, etc.

Cities, Towns and Villages
(Except for scales of 1:20,000,000 or smaller)

PARIS — 1,000,000 and over

Ufa — 500,000 to 1,000,000

Győr — 50,000 to 500,000

Agadir — 25,000 to 50,000

Moreno — 0 to 25,000

TŌKYŌ — National Capitals

Boise — Secondary Capitals

Transportation

Railroads

Railroad Ferries

Caravan Routes

Other Cultural Features

Dams

Pipelines

▲ Pyramids

∴ Ruins

LAND FEATURES

△ Peaks, Spot Heights

= Passes

WATER FEATURES

Lakes and Reservoirs

Fresh Water

Fresh Water: Intermittent

Salt Water

Salt Water: Intermittent

Other Water Features

Swamps

Glaciers

Rivers

Canals

Aqueduct — Aqueducts

Ship Channels

Falls

Rapids

Springs

Water Depths

Sand Bars

Reefs

Europe
Terrain

Europe

Sixth largest continent

•

Third in population: 712,100,000

•

32 cities with over 2 million population

•

Highest mountain: El'brus, 18,510 feet (5,642 meters)

•

Rome and Chicago are the same latitude

Many parts of Europe lie under the shadows of towering mountains. The most splendid of these peaks are the Alps, which make up a mountain range that winds through Switzerland, southeastern France, Austria, southern Germany, northern Italy, and eastward into Slovenia. Three other mountain ranges spread out from the central mass of the Alps into other countries.

Across the English Channel from mainland Europe are the islands that form the United Kingdom. England lies on the biggest island, and central mountains called the Pennines run through that country like a bumpy backbone.

Northern mainland Europe

© Rand McNally & Co.
X-550000-779-1-1-1-2

has many mountains. The uplands of Norway and Sweden are bleak and barren. Long ago huge rivers of ice called *glaciers* ground their way across this land, carving deep grooves in between the mountains. The grooves flooded with water from the sea and have become long waterways called *fjords*. Far to the east the Ural Mountains in Russia mark the division between Europe and Asia. To the southwest of the Alps, the Pyrenees separate France and Spain. Spain and Portugal lie on a *peninsula*, a body of land that is almost surrounded by water.

Many famous rivers flow from Europe's mountains. Perhaps the best known, the Rhine, flows north out of Switzerland, past France, and through Germany and the Netherlands. The Danube is another large river that flows through Germany.

The north-central part of Europe is a fertile area known as the Great European Plain. The rich farmlands of this region supply food for much of Europe, and its minerals help to make the Ruhr Valley on the Rhine River a world center for heavy industry.

Many islands lie to the south of mainland Europe in the Mediterranean Sea. They include Corsica, Sardinia, Sicily, and the isles of Greece. The warm, sunny beaches of the Mediterranean are popular with tourists.

County Kerry, in the southwest corner of Ireland, features green pastures and rugged coastlines.

The rugged, snow capped peaks of the Swiss Alps provide a splendid background for skiers. Tourism is an important part of Switzerland's economy.

Mykonos, shown here, and the other Greek islands in the Aegean Sea are part of the Pindus Mountains. Millions of years ago, a rising sea covered all but the mountain peaks.

Caspian Sea

EUROPE
Animals

Skua

Herring

Barnacle Goose

Reindeer

Wolverine

Grey Seal

Lemming

Hare

Red Deer

Basking Shark

Otter

Black Grouse

Badger

Pheasant

Hedgehog

Atlantic Salmon

Rabbit

Fox

Red-legged Partridge

Chamois

Moorhen

Stork

Marmot

Squirrel

Great Bustard

Barbary Ape

Sole

Ferruginous Duck

Hoopoe

Spanish Mackerel

Raven

Whimbrel

Brown Bear

Pine Marten

Wild Boar

Wolf

Griffon Vulture

Roe Deer

Lesser Spotted Eagle

Tur

Octopus

Conger Eel

Most of the vast, animal-filled forests that once covered much of Europe were cut down long ago to make room for farms, cities, and towns. Many of Europe's animals were hunted for centuries until they were wiped out. But in the few wild places that remain—mostly national parks and game preserves where animals are protected—some of the animals that once abounded in Europe can still be found.

Shaggy wild boars with curved tusks can be found in the forests of central Europe. Packs of wolves still live in some places, and in northern Russia, the huge brown bear still lumbers about.

Many smaller types of animals live in Europe. Foxes, badgers, moles, rabbits, and squirrels are found in many places. Plump little lemmings abound in the mountains of Norway and Sweden. The hedgehog is common in northern Europe.

Small, striped wildcats prowl in parts of eastern Europe. A rather large wildcat, the Spanish lynx, lives in Spain. Three feet (0.91 meter) long with pointed ears and thick whiskers, the lynx is a fast, fierce hunter.

Sparrows, thrushes, finches, nightingales, and ravens are found throughout central Europe. So are large birds of prey such as falcons and eagles. During the summer, the big white stork is a common sight in cities of the Netherlands, Belgium, and Germany, where it nests on the chimneys of houses.

In a protected forest of Poland about 1,600 *wisents*, bison of prehistoric Europe, feed in grassy clearings just as they did thousands of years ago. They stand up to six feet (1.82 meters) high at the shoulder.

EUROPE
Life on the Land

Fishing

Hydrothermal Plant

Reindeer Herding

Coal Mining

Lumbering

Fishing

Agricultural Area

Fishing

Canneries

Papermaking

Dairyland

Fishing

Offshore Oil Drilling

Cheese Making

Dairyland

Troika
(3-horse Sleigh)

Agricultural Area

Agricultural Area

Heavy Industry

Heavy Industry (Steel)

Farming

Houses of Parliament

Bulb Farming

Dairyland

Grimm's Fairy Tale
Country

Eiffel Tower

Oil Fields

Vineyards

Citrus Groves

Export by Sea

Matterhorn

Light
Industry

Wheatlands

Cork Harvesting

Sheep Raised

Olive Orchards

Bullfighting

Water Sports

Roman Ruins

Olive Orchards

Olive Orchards

Opera

Vineyards

Fishing

Vineyards

Ancient Greek Ruins

The whole continent of Europe juts off of Asia and into the sea. No part of western Europe is more than three hundred miles from the sea. It is no wonder that many Europeans depend on fishing or sailing to make their living.

Between the many mountains of Europe lie most of Europe's farms. More than half of the land of Europe is used for farming. The raising of livestock is also important throughout Europe.

Modern industry, especially mining and manufacturing, began in Europe. Today, many world industrial leaders are European nations.

Europe's island nations, Iceland, Ireland, and Great Britain, are no less a part of the continent. The United Kingdom unites the four regions known as England, Scotland, Wales (together called Great Britain), and Northern Ireland. Climate limits agriculture, but the use of mechanized farming methods allows the nation to produce half its food supply.

The northern countries of Europe contain fewer people than the rest of the continent. The thick forests provide these countries with an important resource: wood. All three nations export pulp, paper, furniture, and other wood products.

Europe is smaller than any other continent except Australia. But it has more people than any other continent except for Asia. As a result, Europe is very densely populated.

EUROPE
Countries and Cities

Europe has seen many wars, most of them fought over pieces of land. Thus the boundaries of countries have shifted many times over the centuries. In the 1990s, East and West Germany reunited to again form a single Germany.

The republics that were part of the Soviet Union gained independence and Czechoslovakia divided to form the Czech Republic and Slovakia.

Usually, the borders of countries form around natural barriers, such as rivers, seas, or

mountain ranges. The reason for this is that these are places where people can easily defend themselves from attack. Many European nations are edged by such natural borders.

Today, most European countries elect their leaders. In

some countries, the descendants of the kings and queens that ruled most European countries in earlier times are still treated as royalty, but they do not rule the country.

Travelers to Europe must deal with the continent's many languages. Latin-speaking Romans once conquered much of Europe; today the French, Italians, Spanish, Portuguese, and Romanians speak different tongues—the so-called *Romance* languages—that are based on the ancient Latin. The people of Germany, the Netherlands, England, Denmark, Sweden, and Norway speak languages rooted in a single, ancient tongue—the German of the tribes that occupied those areas in ages past. To the east, the peoples of Poland, the Czech Republic, Slovakia, Bulgaria, and other eastern European nations speak languages based on Slavic dialects.

Europe has many big cities that are rich in history and culture. Rome, Italy, and Athens, Greece, were known thousands of years ago. Paris dates back more than two thousand years. It was founded around 52 B.C. by soldiers of the Roman Empire. Trondheim, in Norway, had its beginning around A.D. 998.

The city of Paris and its surrounding area make up the second largest metropolitan area in Europe. The Eiffel Tower, shown here, has become a symbol of French achievement.

Roads
Railroads

40,000 SQ MI
AREA

0   100   200
Miles

Cities,
Towns,
and
Villages

| 0 to 25,000 ∘ | 100,000 to 250,000 ⊙ | 1,000,000 and over ⊛ |
| 25,000 to 100,000 • | 250,000 to 1,000,000 ⊚ | Major urbanized area |

0 50 100   200   300   400   500 Miles
0   100   200   400   600   800 Kilometers

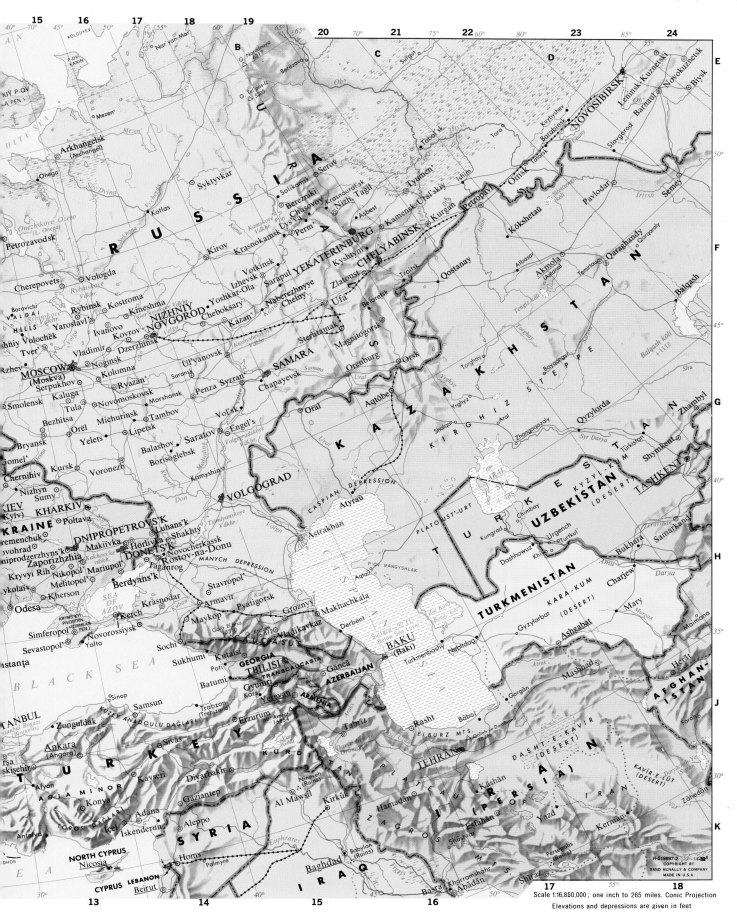

Scale 1:16,850,000 ; one inch to 265 miles. Conic Projection

Elevations and depressions are given in feet

ATLANTIC OCEAN

ARCTIC

BARENTS SEA

KARSKOYE (Kara Sea)

WHITE SEA

NORTH SEA

BALTIC SEA

BLACK SEA

CASPIAN SEA

ARAL SEA

UNITED KINGDOM — GLASGOW, Edinburgh, Aberdeen, Newcastle

Bergen, Trondheim, Oslo — NORWAY

SWEDEN — STOCKHOLM, Göteborg, Norrköping

Turku, Helsinki — FINLAND, LAPLAND

DENMARK — COPENHAGEN, Ålborg, Kiel, Malmö

GERMANY — HAMBURG, BERLIN, Poznań

POLAND — WARSAW, Gdańsk, Łódź, Kraków, Ostrava, Wrocław

Kaliningrad

LITHUANIA — Vilnius, Kaunas

LATVIA — Riga

ESTONIA — Tallinn, Tartu

BELARUS — Minsk, Mogilev, Vitebsk, Gomel, Baranovichi, Brest

Murmansk, Polyarnyy, Kirovsk, KOLA PEN.

ST. PETERSBURG (Leningrad)

Vyborg, Pskov, Novgorod

Petrozavodsk, Arkhangelsk (Archangel)

Syktyvkar, Ust'-Kulom

MOSCOW (Moskva)

Tver, Yaroslavl, Rybinsk, Kostroma, Ivanovo, Vladimir, Ryazan', Tula, Kaluga, Smolensk, Bryansk, Orël, Kursk, Voronezh, Lipetsk, Tambov, Penza, Saratov

NIZHNIY NOVGOROD

Kirov, Perm', Izhevsk, Kazan', Glazov

YEKATERINBURG, Nizhniy Tagil, Chelyabinsk

SAMARA, Ufa, Sterlitamak, Magnitogorsk, Orenburg, Orsk

UKRAINE — KIEV (Kyïv), KHARKIV, DNIPROPETROVSK, DONETS'K, Odesa, Kryvyi Rih, Zaporizhzhia, Mykolaïv, Poltava, Sumy, Zhytomyr, Vinnytsia, Chernivtsi, L'viv, Ivano-Frankivs'k

MOLD. — Chişinău

Simferopol', Sevastopol', Kerch, Mariupol', Rostov-na-Donu, Krasnodar, Novorossiysk, Sochi, Stavropol', Armavir, Volgograd, Astrakhan

CAUCASUS

GEORGIA — Tbilisi, Batumi

ARMENIA — Yerevan

AZERBAIJAN — BAKU (Bakı), Gäncä

TURKEY — Samsun, Trabzon, Sivas, Erzurum, Erzincan, Malatya, Diyarbakir, Kars

KURDISTAN

IRAQ — Baghdad, Kirkūk, Al Mawsil

IRAN — TEHRAN, Tabrīz, Rasht, Zanjān, Hamadān, Bakhtārān, Eşfahān, Kāshān, Mashhad, Emāmshahr

ELBURZ MTS., ZAGROS MTS.

TURKMENISTAN — Ashgabat, Turkmenbashy, Dashhowuz, Mary, Gyzylarbat

KARA-KUM (DESERT)

UZBEKISTAN — TASHKENT, Bukhara, Samarkand, Charjew, Nurata, Qarshi, Shakhrisyabz, Türtkul

KYZYL-KUM (DESERT)

TURKESTAN

KAZAKHSTAN — Aqtöbe, Atyraū, Qostanay, Aral, Zhangaqazaly, Qyzylorda, Shymkent, Zhambyl, Balqash, Qaraghandy, Qarqaraly, Semey, Pavlodar, Temirtau, AKMOLA (Astana), Bayanauyl, Ayaköz, Zaysan, Ürzhar, Ushtal, Taldyqorghan

KIRGHIZ STEPPE

CASPIAN DEPRESSION

KYRGYZSTAN — Bishkek, Osh, Pergana, Andizhan, Dzhalal-Abad, Naryn, Tokmak

TAJIK. — Dushanbe

Almaty (Alma-Ata), Przheval'sk

TIEN SHAN

CHINA — Ürümqi, Kashi

WESTERN SIBERIAN LOWLAND

Omsk, NOVOSIBIRSK, Tomsk, Barnaul, Rubtsovsk, Kemerovo, Anzhero-Sudzhensk, Kiselëvsk, Novokuznetsk

Tyumen', Kurgan, Petropavl, Ishim, Tatarsk, Kupino, Slavgorod, Kamen-na-Obi, Kulunda

Surgut, Khanty Mansiysk, Narym, Kolpashevo

Salekhard, Vorkuta, Novyy Port, Tazovskoye, Berezovo

PECHORA BASIN, Ust'-Tsil'ma, Nar'yan-Mar

NOVAYA ZEMLYA, ZEMLYA FRANTSA IOSIFA (FRANZ JOSEF LAND), SVALBARD (SPITSBERGEN, Nor.), ZEMLYA

Scale 1:21,500,000; one inch to 340 miles
Lambert's Azimuthal, Equal Area Projection
Elevations and depressions are given in f...

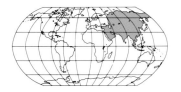

Asia
Terrain

Asia

Largest continent
•
First in population: 3,600,000,000
•
66 cities with over 2 million population
•
World's highest mountain: Everest, 29,028 feet (8,848 meters)
•
World's largest 'lake'': Caspian Sea, 143,240 square miles (370,990 square kilometers)
•
World's lowest inland point: Dead Sea, 1,339 feet (408 meters) below sea level

Asia is the largest continent. It covers more area than North America, Europe, and Australia combined. Because it is so big, it is a land of many extremes. It has some of the world's highest mountains, longest rivers, largest deserts, and coldest and hottest climates.

Asia begins at the Ural Mountains in Russia and extends more than three thousand miles (almost five thousand kilometers), all the way to the Pacific Ocean. This northern region is known as Siberia.

To the south of Siberia is an equally large, equally harsh region. This area begins in the deserts of Saudi Arabia and sweeps across central Asia through Iraq, Iran, into Turkmenistan and Kazakhstan, through parts of China, and on into the deserts of Mongolia.

The region is bounded in the south by the highest mountains on the earth: the Himalayas. The mountains thrust up when the Indian subcontinent crashed into Asia millions of years ago. The two peaks that are considered the highest in the world, Mount Everest and K2, are in the Himalayas.

The erosion of limestone created this unusual cone-shaped hill near Guilin in southeastern China. Regions such as these are called *karst*. Images of karst can often be found in traditional Chinese art.

In northern Pakistan, apricots grown in the rugged terrain and harsh climate of the Himalayas dry in the sun. The highest mountains in the world, the Himalayas stretch some 1,550 miles (2,500 kilometers) across central Asia and cut across five countries.

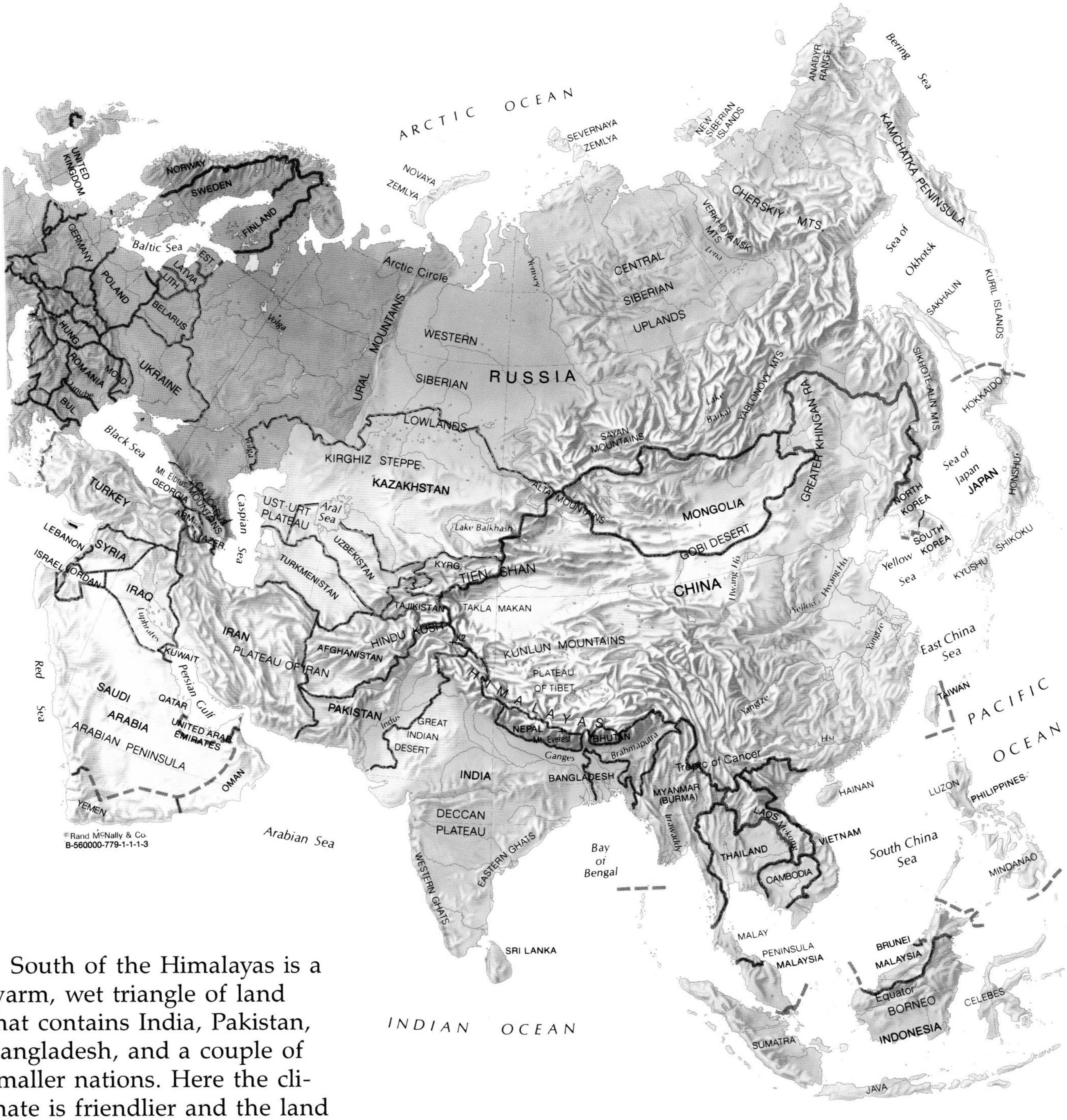

The map labels, arranged roughly by region:

ARCTIC OCEAN

UNITED KINGDOM
NORWAY
SWEDEN
FINLAND
Baltic Sea
GERMANY
POLAND
BELARUS
LATVIA
LITH.
EST.
UKRAINE
HUNG.
ROMANIA
MOLD.
BUL.
Danube
Black Sea
Volga

SEVERNAYA ZEMLYA
NOVAYA ZEMLYA
Arctic Circle
NEW SIBERIAN ISLANDS
Bering Sea
KAMCHATKA PENINSULA
ANADYR RANGE

URAL MOUNTAINS
WESTERN SIBERIAN LOWLANDS
CENTRAL SIBERIAN UPLANDS
RUSSIA
Yenisey
Lena
Ob
CHERSKIY MTS.
VERKHOYANSK MTS.
Sea of Okhotsk
SAKHALIN
KURIL ISLANDS

KIRGHIZ STEPPE
KAZAKHSTAN
Aral Sea
UST-URT PLATEAU
Caspian Sea
SAYAN MOUNTAINS
ALTAI MOUNTAINS
Lake Baikal
YABLONOVYY MTS.
GREATER KHINGAN RA.
SIKHOTE-ALIN MTS.
HOKKAIDO
Sea of Japan
JAPAN
HONSHU

TURKEY
GEORGIA
ARM.
AZER.
Mt. Elbrus
CAUCASUS MOUNTAINS
Lake Balkhash
TURKMENISTAN
UZBEKISTAN
KYRG.
TIEN SHAN
MONGOLIA
GOBI DESERT
Hwang Ho
NORTH KOREA
SOUTH KOREA
Yellow Sea
SHIKOKU
KYUSHU

LEBANON
SYRIA
ISRAEL
JORDAN
IRAQ
Euphrates
Tigris
KUWAIT
IRAN
PLATEAU OF IRAN
TAJIKISTAN
HINDU KUSH
K2
TAKLA MAKAN
KUNLUN MOUNTAINS
CHINA
Yangtze
Nen
Hsi
EAST CHINA SEA
TAIWAN
PACIFIC OCEAN

Red Sea
SAUDI ARABIA
QATAR
UNITED ARAB EMIRATES
Persian Gulf
AFGHANISTAN
PAKISTAN
Indus
PLATEAU OF TIBET
HIMALAYAS
NEPAL
Mt. Everest
BHUTAN
Brahmaputra
Ganges
HAINAN
LUZON
PHILIPPINES

ARABIAN PENINSULA
OMAN
YEMEN
Arabian Sea
GREAT INDIAN DESERT
INDIA
BANGLADESH
MYANMAR (BURMA)
Irrawaddy
LAOS
Mekong
VIETNAM
South China Sea
MINDANAO

DECCAN PLATEAU
WESTERN GHATS
EASTERN GHATS
Bay of Bengal
Tropic of Cancer
THAILAND
CAMBODIA

SRI LANKA
INDIAN OCEAN
MALAY PENINSULA
MALAYSIA
BRUNEI
MALAYSIA
Equator
BORNEO
CELEBES
SUMATRA
INDONESIA
JAVA

©Rand McNally & Co.
B-560000-779-1-1-1-3

South of the Himalayas is a warm, wet triangle of land that contains India, Pakistan, Bangladesh, and a couple of smaller nations. Here the climate is friendlier and the land more fertile, so many people live in this area. In fact, this is one of the world's most crowded regions.

To the east lies Southeast Asia, a land that is a giant rain forest. It is very fertile and has plenty of rainfall. These factors make Southeast Asia a good place to live, so the countries of this region are highly populated.

North of Southeast Asia is an area known as the Far East. It includes most of China, North Korea, South Korea, and Japan. Many people live in these countries. In fact, China holds more people—over one billion—than any other country in the world.

The four main Japanese islands are part of a chain of recently formed volcanic mountains. Mountains cover two-thirds of the country.

Animals

Asia spreads from far northern lands covered with snow nine months a year to the steamy, hot rain forests that skirt the equator. This wide range of environments provides habitats for an enormous variety of animals.

Large white polar bears leap among the ice floes in the northernmost Siberian coasts. Reindeer, foxes, hares, and tiny, mouselike lemmings live in northern Asia. In northern China and Korea lives the thick-furred Siberian tiger, completely at home in cold and snow.

The forests of southern Asia swarm with animals—monkeys, tree-dwelling leopards, small herds of wild cattle called gaurs, and an ever-dwindling number of tigers. Indian elephants move through the forests in herds numbering from ten to fifty.

The deadly king cobra, the world's longest poisonous snake, also makes the forest its home. Its bite can kill a human within fifteen minutes. The cobra's enemy, the mongoose, also lives in the Asian forests. The fast, clever mongoose will attack and eat a cobra—or any other snake—on sight.

In the high bamboo forests in part of central China lives the giant panda. Mostly white with black legs, ears, and eye patches, this gentle bear-like creature is active mostly at night. The smaller red panda, which looks something like a raccoon, can be found in the Himalayas and the mountains of western China and northern Myanmar (Burma).

Imperial Eagle

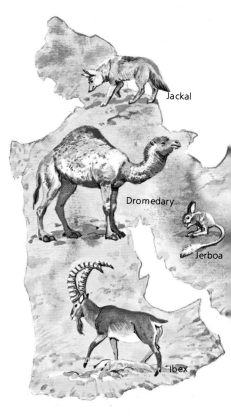

Jackal

Dromedary

Jerboa

Ibex

The largest horns grown by any animal are those of a sheep called the Pamir argali, or Marco Polo's argali. Marco Polo found this unusual creature during his travels across central Asia. The sheep's horns spiral outward and have been known to reach seventy-five inches (190.5 centimeters).

Polar Bear

Killer Whale

Arctic Fox

Willow Grouse

Sea Eagle

Elk

Snowy Owl

Wolf

Harbor Seal

Lynx

Przewalski's Horse

Raccoon-like Dog

Japanese Macaque

Saiga

Yak

Giant Panda

Bactrian Camel

Mandarin Duck

Japanese Crane

Snow Leopard

Pheasant

Water Buffalo

Dolphin

Indian Elephant

Tiger

Cormorant

Flyingfish

Peafowl

Gibbon

Cobra

Orangutan

Macaque

Mongoose

ASIA
Life on the Land

More than half the earth's people live on the vast continent of Asia. Throughout the world, people naturally tend to live in areas where the climate and land are good for producing food. About two-thirds of Asia's population make their living by farming, and the continent's agricultural areas are among its most crowded.

In much of China, Japan, India, and the tropical lands of Southeast Asia, the most important crop is rice. It is the main food of many Asian people, and Asia produces most of the world's rice. Cotton is the main crop of parts of southwestern Asia, also known as the Middle East.

The land of northern Asia is too cold for much farming, and the soil in central Asia is not good for growing crops. In these regions, some people raise cattle and sheep.

Petroleum, or crude oil, is a precious substance in today's world. Beneath the deserts of the Middle East lie some of the world's greatest oil reserves. The countries of this region sell, or *export*, oil to many other countries around the world.

There is not much industry in most of Asia, but there is a lot in Israel, China, and western Russia. Industry in South Korea, Taiwan, Singapore, and Hong Kong is growing rapidly. Japan, which has few natural resources, continues to be a leader in world industry, producing automobiles, chemicals, and electronic equipment.

The Arabs of the Middle East tell a story about a young boy named Aladdin, who finds an old lamp. When he rubs the lamp, a genie appears and grants him three wishes.

Agricultural Area

Truck Farming

Vineyards

Sheep Raised

Jerusalem

Oil Fields

Dates

Farming by Irrigation

The Indonesian island of Bali, off of Southeast Asia, is known for its folk dances. One, called the *legong*, tells an ancient story of love and battle. Each movement has a meaning and tells a part of the story.

Mining

Fur Trapping

Logging

Truck Farming

Reindeer Herds

Mining

Rice Grown

Mining

Smelting of Ore

Truck Farming

Logging

Light and Heavy Industry

Cossack Dancer

Wheatlands

Tea Grown

Wheatlands

Great Wall of China

Steel Manufactured

Hydroelectric Power

Sheep Raised

Gate of Heavenly Peace

Farming

Citrus Fruits Grown

Smelting of Ore

Chinese Junk

Goods Shipped by Caravan

Traditional Chinese Urn

Agricultural Area

Ruins of Persepolis, Persia

Palace of the Dalai Lama

Agricultural Area

Persian Carpet

Corn

Cacao (Chocolate)

Cotton

Wheat

Manufacturing

Bathing in the Sacred Ganges

Coconuts

Mt. Everest

Taj Mahal

Burmese Temples

Fishing

Rice Grown

Logging

Oil

Tea Grown

Coconuts

Agricultural Area

Fishing

Rubber

Teak

Coffee

ASIA
Countries and Cities

The nations of immense Asia tended to form in clusters. The continent has five large groupings of nations. The first, which borders the eastern edge of the continent, is called the Far East and its leading countries include China and Japan. Indochina and the islands of Indonesia make up the second group, and a third formed within the triangle of land that contains India. The desert countries make up a fourth cluster. Siberia, a part of the Soviet Union, stands alone as the fifth.

China holds the most people of any nation—over one billion. One out of every five persons on earth is Chinese! Asia's industrial giant is Japan.

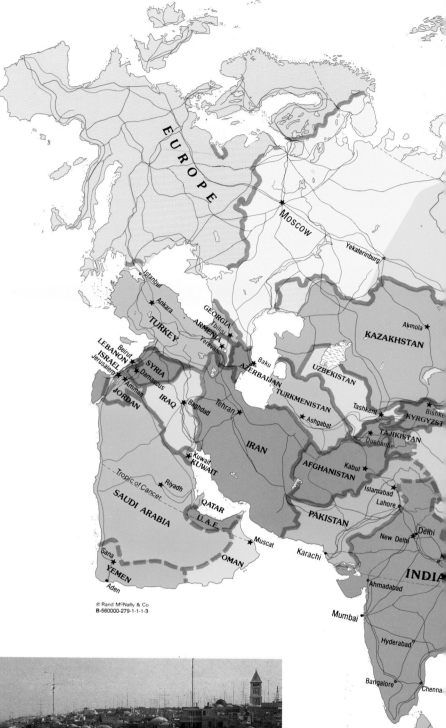

© Rand McNally & Co
B-560000-279-1-1-1-3

With a history of more than five thousand years, Jerusalem has long been a holy city of Christianity, Judaism, and Islam. The city, divided after one war and reunified in another, was declared Israel's permanent capital in 1980.

Today, after a rapid rise following defeat in World War II, Japan's industrial muscle is exceeded only by the United States and the Soviet Union.

The second cluster of countries occurs in Indochina. Many of the nations of Indochina formed around river valleys where food grows well. Burma (Myanmar) formed around the Irrawaddy River, and Thailand around the Menam. Cambodia and Vietnam share the lower Mekong River, while Laos grew around the northern part.

India, Pakistan, Bangladesh, and Sri Lanka, countries of the third grouping, struggle with poverty. Nearly 837 million people live in India, giving it a population second only to China's. Neighboring Bangladesh has fertile lands, but poor farming methods keep rice in short supply.

The fourth cluster of Asian nations lies on the deserts. Fewer people live here. Turkey, with more farmland than other countries in the region, has just sixty-three million people. Only in Israel, established in 1948 as a Jewish homeland, does the population density approach that of European countries.

Siberia, the fifth region of Asia, is part of the Soviet Union. Its people are few and far between. One-third of the Soviet Union's coal comes from the industrialized Kuznetsk Basin area, which also produces building materials, chemicals, and machinery.

Roads
Railroads

Scale 1:42,000,000; one inch to 665 miles. Lambert's Azimuthal, Equal Area Projection
Elevations and depressions are given in feet

40,000 SQ MI AREA

0   300   600
Miles

H-519695-26 19-18 41°
COPYRIGHT BY
RAND MCNALLY & COMPANY
MADE IN U.S.A.

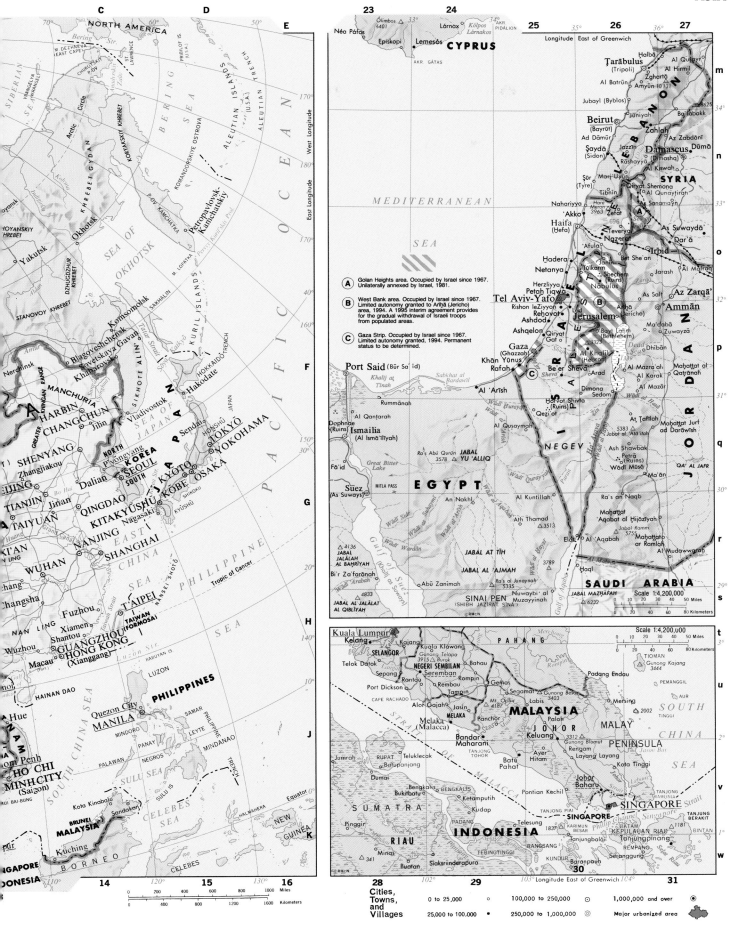

Africa
Terrain

Africa

Second largest continent
•
Second in population: 759,800,000
•
16 cities with over 2 million population
•
Highest mountain: Kilimanjaro,
19,340 feet (5,895 meters)
•
World's largest desert: Sahara,
approximately 3,500,000 square miles
(9,065,000 square kilometers)
•
World's longest river system: Nile,
4,145 miles (6,671 kilometers)
•
World's highest recorded temperature:
Azizia, Libya, 136.4°F (58°C)
•
Equator passes through

The continent of Africa is second in size only to Asia. Yet few people realize just how huge it is. For example, the entire continental United States (which excludes Alaska and Hawaii) could be tucked comfortably into the Sahara Desert, which extends 3,200 miles (5,150 kilometers) across northern Africa.

Many people imagine Africa as a land of rain forests. In reality, most of Africa is covered with desert or grassland. The Sahara takes up most of northern Africa; the Kalahari and Namib deserts lie in the south. Between these two desert regions are many, many miles of grassland called *savanna*. Rain forests, following the equator, mainly occupy the middle of the continent.

Africa has some magnificent mountains, but it lacks the huge chains common to most of the other continents. The Atlas Mountains arch across the top of Africa, through Morocco, Algeria, and Tunisia, forming a barrier between the northern coast and the Sahara. They were raised over thirty million years ago, at the same time as the Alps of Europe.

In East Africa, mountain peaks follow two nearly parallel straight lines. Among the eastern mountains, snow-capped Mount Kilimanjaro, Africa's highest peak, soars to more than nineteen thousand feet.

Shown here is the type of grassland, called savanna, that covers much of Africa. This particular scene is in the nation of Zambia.

Africa's Great Rift Valley extends about four thousand miles (almost 6,500 kilometers). It can be traced along the many lakes and seas that fill parts of it. The cutaway at right shows some of those bodies of water.

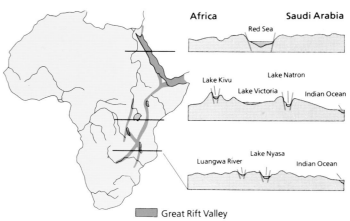

Great Rift Valley

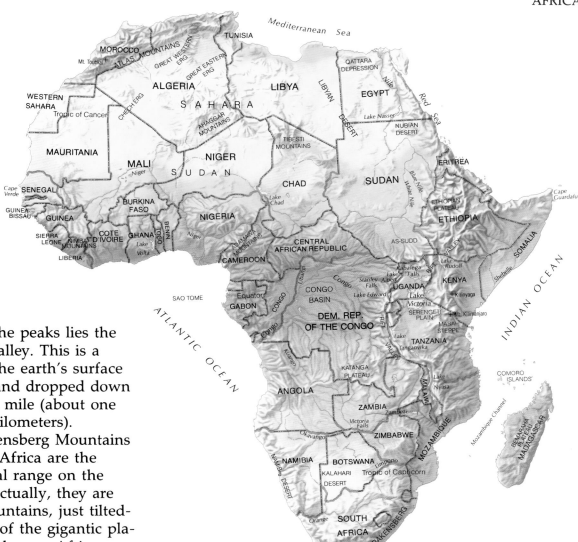

Between the peaks lies the Great Rift Valley. This is a long rip in the earth's surface where the land dropped down more than a mile (about one and a half kilometers).

The Drakensberg Mountains in southern Africa are the most unusual range on the continent. Actually, they are not true mountains, just tilted-up portions of the gigantic plateau that makes up Africa.

Four important rivers flow out of Africa. The Niger runs through several West African countries and out into the Atlantic Ocean. The Congo flows west out of central Africa. The Zambezi, toward southern Africa, flows east to the Indian Ocean. And finally, the great Nile flows northward through several countries, including Egypt, and empties into the Mediterranean Sea. The Nile is the longest river in the world.

Palm trees line the shore along the Gulf of Guinea, which lies to the south of Ghana. This coastal region sports white-sand beaches and blue lagoons.

AFRICA
Animals

Africa is a continent of rain forests, grassy plains, and deserts. Each environment holds different types of animals that have adapted to the conditions. Many African animals are beautiful creatures, but some of these magnificent beasts are in danger of becoming extinct.

In the north the enormous Sahara Desert spreads across thousands of miles. Not many animals can live in that wasteland, and those that do are able to survive with little or no water.

The best-known animal of the Sahara is the one-humped Arabian camel, also known as the dromedary. All camels in the Sahara are used as tame beasts of burden.

The great rain forest of central Africa straddles the equator. Within it roam bands of chimpanzees, which live on fruit and tender plants. The gorilla also lives here, a shy and gentle animal despite its size. Here, too, are found buffalo, leopards, many kinds of monkeys, and the little okapi, a brown-bodied animal with striped legs.

The vast, grassy plains that lie north and south of the central rain forests contain many of the continent's best-known animals. Herds of African elephants, the largest of all land animals, rumble across through the plains. The spotted cheetah, swiftest of all animals, prowls the grasslands in search of prey. It must compete with an even more famous cat, however, for the African lion, a symbol of pride and power, also hunts in the African plains.

Tarpon

Addax

Fennec

Pangolin

Colobus Monkey

Despite their fearsome appearance, gorillas are gentle beasts who eat only plants. Like many African animals, gorillas are threatened with extinction—a result of being hunted and losing their rain forest habitat.

Jackal

Dromedary

Crowned Crane

Eared Vulture

Dorcas Gazelle

Barbary Sheep

Striped Hyena

Crocodile

Greater Kudu

Aardvark

Elephant

Giraffe

Baboon

Chimpanzee

Gorilla

Leopard

Black Rhinoceros

Hornbill

Cape Buffalo

Hippopotamus

White Pelican

Eland

Zebra

Lion

Tenrec

Python

Chameleon

Wildebeest

Ring-tailed Lemur

Cheetah

Impala

Angelfish

Ostrich

Sacred Ibis

AFRICA
Life on the Land

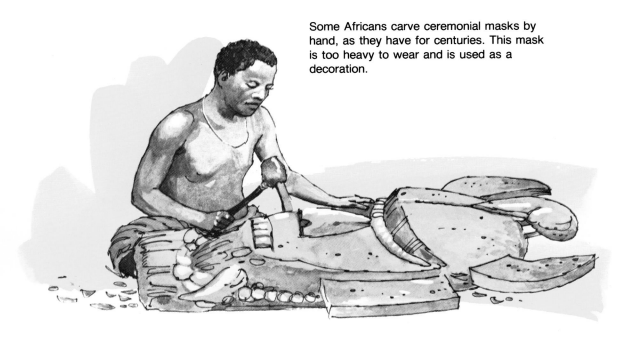

Some Africans carve ceremonial masks by hand, as they have for centuries. This mask is too heavy to wear and is used as a decoration.

Agricultural Area

Peanuts

Chocolate

Most Africans are either farmers or herders. Many of them live as their ancestors did for thousands of years. They roam the land for food or live in tiny villages, raising crops and animals mostly for their own use and not for sale to other countries.

Little farming can be done in hot, dry North Africa. But along the coasts of Morocco, Algeria, and Tunisia, farmers can grow a few crops—such as citrus fruits, grapes, almonds, grains, and olives.

Drilling for oil is important to several African countries. Algeria and Libya in the north and the nations of Nigeria and Gabon farther south export oil and natural gas to other countries.

West Africa is an important agricultural area. Among other crops, people here grow cacao beans, from which chocolate and cocoa are made. The forests of central Africa produce rubber trees and banana trees. In East Africa, herding cattle has been the main way of life for many years.

Farther south, in the country of South Africa, the fertile land is farmed by the descendants of Europeans who settled there many years ago. The land of South Africa also holds many minerals, such as platinum, antimony, chromium, and manganese. Most of the world's diamonds—both gems and those used in industry—and much of its gold come from South African mines. This vast mineral wealth helped build South Africa into the continent's most industrialized nation.

Ananse the Spider Man is a character in a famous African tale. Ananse gathered all the wisdom in the world into a huge pot and tried to keep it for himself. But the pot fell as Ananse tried to hide it in a tree, and all the wisdom blew away.

Agricultural Area

Moorish-style Architecture

Corn

Fishing

Vineyards

Wheat

Olives

Cairo

Tobacco

Sphinx

Nomad with Goats

Oil Fields

Dates Harvested

The Great Pyramid at Giza

Cotton Grown

Goods Shipped by Caravan

Cotton Made into Cloth

Leather Products Made

Sand Dunes

African Village

Cattle Raised

Sheep Raised

Rubber

Palm Oil

Mining

Plantains (African Bananas)

Tourists Welcomed

Cattle Raised

Cacao Beans (Chocolate)

Copra (Dried Coconut) Shipped

Central Forests

Oil Fields

Mt. Kilimanjaro

Pygmy

Agricultural Area

Minerals Mined

Masai Tribesman

Corn

Coal Mines

Tea

Victoria Falls

Diamond Mines

Citrus Fruits

Sheep Raised

Yams

Vanilla Beans Grown

Gold Mines

AFRICA
Countries and Cities

Human history began in Africa. Scientists believe that the earliest human beings walked the grasslands of East Africa about two million years ago. Over many years, humans migrated out of Africa to inhabit other parts of the world.

Civilization has a long history in North Africa. The Nile Valley of Egypt cradled the center of one of the world's oldest civilizations, which developed over five thousand years ago. Some of the cities of Egypt, including Alexandria and Cairo, are more than one thousand years old. Cairo is

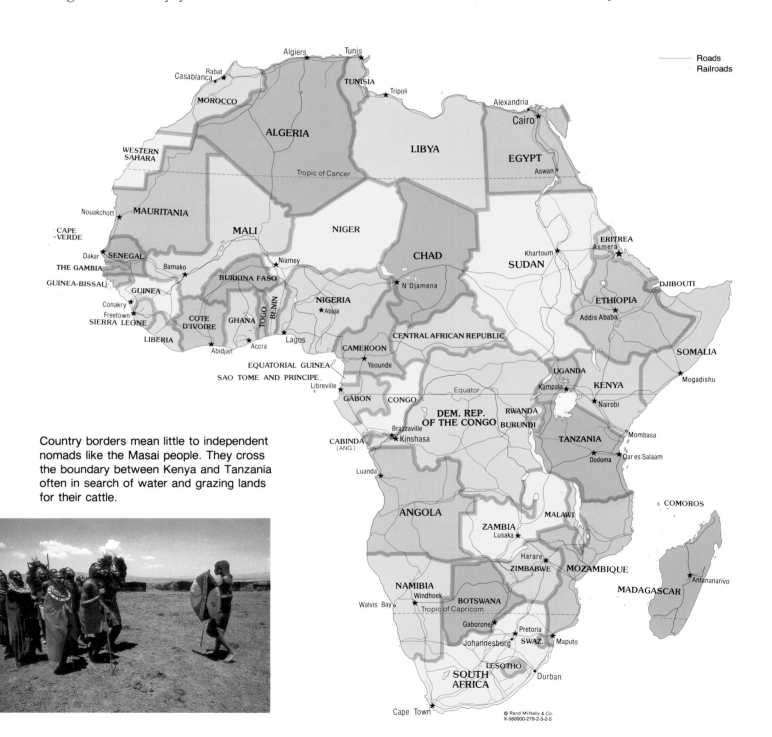

Country borders mean little to independent nomads like the Masai people. They cross the boundary between Kenya and Tanzania often in search of water and grazing lands for their cattle.

Roads
Railroads

Algiers · Tunis · Rabat · Casablanca · MOROCCO · TUNISIA · Tripoli · Alexandria · Cairo · ALGERIA · LIBYA · EGYPT · WESTERN SAHARA · Tropic of Cancer · Aswan · Nouakchott · MAURITANIA · MALI · NIGER · CAPE VERDE · Dakar · SENEGAL · Bamako · KHARTOUM · ERITREA · Asmera · THE GAMBIA · BURKINA FASO · CHAD · SUDAN · GUINEA-BISSAU · GUINEA · Niamey · DJIBOUTI · Conakry · Freetown · SIERRA LEONE · NIGERIA · N'Djamena · ETHIOPIA · COTE D'IVOIRE · GHANA · TOGO · BENIN · Abuja · Addis Ababa · LIBERIA · Abidjan · Accra · Lagos · CENTRAL AFRICAN REPUBLIC · SOMALIA · CAMEROON · Mogadishu · EQUATORIAL GUINEA · Yaounde · SAO TOME AND PRINCIPE · Libreville · UGANDA · KENYA · Equator · Kampala · GABON · CONGO · Nairobi · DEM. REP. OF THE CONGO · RWANDA · BURUNDI · Brazzaville · Mombasa · CABINDA (ANG.) · Kinshasa · TANZANIA · Dodoma · Dar es Salaam · Luanda · COMOROS · ANGOLA · MALAWI · ZAMBIA · Lusaka · Harare · ZIMBABWE · MOZAMBIQUE · MADAGASCAR · Antananarivo · NAMIBIA · Windhoek · BOTSWANA · Walvis Bay · Tropic of Capricorn · Gaborone · Pretoria · Johannesburg · SWAZ. · Maputo · LESOTHO · Durban · SOUTH AFRICA · Cape Town

© Rand McNally & Co.
X-580000-279-2-3-2-5

Tunisia's population is concentrated along the coast, but village scenes such as this one are common in the nation's semi-arid mountain regions. Most of the inhabitants of these central and southern areas live in houses of stone and mud.

In many African nations, the capital city is the only sizable urban center. Harare, pictured here, is the capital and largest city of Zimbabwe, in southern Africa.

also the biggest city in Africa.

During the seventh century A.D., the religion of Islam was adopted throughout much of North Africa. Beautiful Muslim mosques were built in what is now Libya, Algeria, Tunisia, and Morocco.

By the 1400s, Europeans began sailing to Africa and conquering the peoples who lived there. The Europeans were interested mainly in profiting from the vast resources they found in Africa. By the early 1900s, almost all of Africa was under European rule. The borders of many African countries were set up by European colonists who settled there. Most of the European governments are gone now, replaced by the independent nations.

Much of West Africa is a hot, moist, lowland area. In past centuries raiders visited these shores, kidnaped people, carried them away in ships, and sold them as laborers throughout the world. Today, more than one-fourth of the people in Africa live in these western nations. Nigeria, with over 91 million people, is Africa's most populous country.

The equator passes through central Africa. The Democratic Republic of the Congo is the biggest country in the region, holding thirty-five million people.

Mountains and the Great Rift Valley separate East Africa from the rest of the continent. Here are grasslands on which groups of people herd cattle and many wild animals roam. Kenya and Tanzania have set aside vast areas where the animals are protected.

AÇORES (AZORES) (Port.)
GRACIOSA
TERCEIRA
FAIAL
PICO
SÃO JORGE
SÃO MIGUEL
Ponta Delgada
STA. MARIA
Same scale as main map
©RMCN

SPAIN
Cádiz
Str. of Gibraltar
Gibraltar (U. K.)
Ceuta (Sp.)
Tanger (Tangier)
Tetouan
Melilla (Sp.)
Larache
Ech Cheliff
Delles
Bejaïa (Bougie)
El Milyya
Skikda
Annaba (Bône)
Tunis
Bizerte
Algiers (El Djazaïr) Cherchel
Tizi-Ouzou
Mestghanem
Oran
Ain el Beida
Batna
Guelma
Constantine
TUNISIA
Souss
Ech Cheliff
Ghilizane
M'Sila
Stif
Tbessa
Sfax
Cekhira
Ghazouane
Ouezzane
Fès
Taza
Oujda
Tilimsen
Saïda
El Djelfa
Aflou
Laghouat
Aïn-Sefra
Ghardaïa
El Wad
Touggourt
Gabès
de Gabès

CASABLANCA
El Jadida
Rabat
Salé
Meknès
Settat
Oued-Zem
Kasba-Tadla
Béchar
Figuig
Igli
Béni Abbas
El Menia
Hassi Messaoud
Daraj
Ghudāmis
AL HA
Al

Safi (Asfi)
Marrakech
Essaouira
Demnat
MOROCCO
ATLAS
Jebel Toubkal 13665
Boudenib

Agadir
Taroudant
GRAND ERG OCCIDENTAL
Timimoun
GRAND ERG ORIENTAL

ATLANTIC OCEAN
Funchal
ILHA DE PORTO SANTO
DA MADEIRA (Port.)
ARQUIPÉLAGO
ILHA DA MADEIRA

Sidi Ifni
Tiznit
ANTI ATLAS
ALGERIA
Adrar
In Salah
Bordj Omar Idriss
In Amnas
PLATEAU DU TADEMAÏT
PLATEAU DU TINGHERT
Illizi
Ghât
Sardal

ISLAS CANARIAS (Sp.)
LANZAROTE
LA PALMA
Sta. Cruz de Tenerife
TENERIFE
FUERTEVENTURA
CAP DRÂA
GOMERA
San Sebastián
Las Palmas de Gran Canaria
GRAN CANARIA
HIERRO
C. YUBY
Oued Drâa

El Aaiún
CABO BOJADOR
ERG IGUIDI
ERG CHECH
TANEZROUFT
Chenachane
TIDIKELT
TASSILI-N-AJJER
Tahat 9541
AHAGGAR
Djanet

The Western Sahara is occupied by Morocco.
WESTERN SAHARA
Tindouf
EL HANK
SAHARA
Ouallene
Tamenghest
TUAREG

Dakhla
Tropic of Cancer
Fdérik
Taoudenni
DJOUF
EL
ADRAR DES IFÔGHAS
Mt. Gréboun 6562
Iferouâne
Monts Tamgak 5906
AÏR
Monts Bagzane 6300

Nouadhibou
CAP BLANC
CAP D'ARGUIN
Atar
Chinguetti
OUARANE
Oued Tamenghest
Kidal

Nouamrhar
CAP TIMIRIS
Akjoujt
EL MREYYÉ
Mabrouk
VALLÉE DU TILEMSI

MAURITANIA
Araouane
NIGER
Nouakchott
Boutilimit
Tidjikdja
MALI
Tombouctou (Timbuktu)
Bamba
Agadez

Saint-Louis
Podor
Aleg
Kiffa
Néma
Oualâta
Goundam
Bourem
Gao
Tahoua

Dagana
Kaédi
Matam
Mbout
Sélibaby
Nioro du Sahel
Nara
Sokolo
Madaoua
Tessaoua
Zinder
Gouré

Louga
Linguère
Goumbou
Mopti
Bandiagara
Tillabéry
Niamey
Dosso
Sokoto
Maradi
Kaura Namoda
Nguru
Geida
BO
PLA

Rufisque
Diourbel
CAP VERT
Dakar
Thiès
Kaolack
SENEGAL
Kayes
Bakel
Ségou
Djenné
San
Dori
Kaya
Say
Katsina
Gumel
Hadejia

THE GAMBIA
Banjul
Tambacounda
Kita
Koulikoro
BURKINA FASO
Ouagadougou
Koudougou
Fada Ngourma
Birnin Kebbi
Gusau
Kano
Gaya

Ziguinchor
GUINEA-BISSAU
Bissau
Bolama
Buba
Boké
Kita
Bamako
Bougouni
Sikasso
Dédougou
Tenkodogo
Malanville
Illo
Kandi
Zaria
Kaduna
Bauchi
Gombe
Potiskum

Bafoulabé
Satadougou
Bakel
Koutiala
Bobo-Dioulasso
Gambaga
Sansanné-Mango
Natitingou
Kontagora
Zungeru
Minna
Jos
Yol
ADAM

FOUTA DJALLON
Labé
Siguiri
Kankan
Odienné
Korhogo
Kong
Yendi
Tamale
Sokodé
Parakou
Jebba
Abuja
NIGERIA

GUINEA
Timbo
Mamou
Kouroussa
Bougouni
KONG
Bouna
Bole
Bondoukou
Savalou
Bida
Baro
Keffi
Ibi

Boffa
Kindia
Faranah
Beyla
Séguéla
Bouaké
Dabakala
Kintampo
TOGO
Iseyin
Oyo
Ilorin
Ogbomosho
Oshogbo
Lokoja
Katsina Ala
GOTEL MTS

Forécariah
Conakry
Kabala
Kissidougou
Bouaflé
Bouaké
GHANA
Abomey
Ibadan
Iwo
Ife
Ilesha
Idah
Makurdi
Kontch

SIERRA LEONE
Freetown
Makeni
Kolahun
Mont Nimba 5760
COTE D'IVOIRE (IVORY COAST)
Yamoussoukro
Kumasi
Koforidua
Iebu Ode
Benin City
Enugu
Onitsha
Aba
Mamfe
Fouman
Dschang

Moyamba
Pendembu
Bomi Hills
Robertsport
Séguéla
Abidjan
Port-Bouët
Accra
Porto-Novo
Lagos
Sapele
Warri
Owerri
Port Harcourt
Calabar
CAMER

Bonthe
Bomi Hills
LIBERIA
Monrovia
Buchanan
River Cess
Greenville
CAPE PALMAS
Harper
Tabou
Grand Lahou
Grand Bassam
Assini
C. THREE POINTS
Sekondi-Takoradi
Saltpond
Cape Coast
Forcados
Brass
Bonny
Kumba
Yaoundé
Douala
Edéa
Eséka

ATLANTIC OCEAN
GULF OF GUINEA
Lake Volta
Bight of Benin
Cameroon Mtn. 13451
Limbe
Malabo
BIOKO
EQUATORIAL GUINEA
Bata
RIO MUNI
Kribi
Bight of Biafra
Campo
Ebolowa
Oyem

SAO TOME AND PRINCIPE
ILHA DO PRINCIPE
ILHA DE SÃO TOMÉ
São Tomé
Libreville
GAB

CAPE VERDE
SANTA ANTÃO
SÃO VICENTE
SAL
SÃO NICOLAU
BOA VISTA
SÃO TIAGO
MAIO
FOGO
Praia
Same scale as main map
©RMCN

X-589100-2E   17-18-35
COPYRIGHT BY
RAND McNALLY & COMPANY
MADE IN U.S.A.

Longitude West of Greenwich
Longitude East of Greenwich

Scale 1:16,850,000; one inch to 265 miles. Sinusoidal Projection
Elevations and depressions are given in feet

Cities, Towns, and Villages

0 to 25,000 ○	100,000 to 250,000 ⊙	1,000,000 and over ◉
25,000 to 100,000 •	250,000 to 1,000,000 ◎	Major urbanized area

7 8 9 10 11 12 13

ITALY
SICILIA (SICILY)
PANTELLERIA (It.)
MALTA
KERKENNA

GREECE
Khaniá
Iráklion
CRETE (KRITI)
RHODES (RODHOS) (GR)

TURKEY
Antalya
Adana
Iskenderun
Hatay
Halab (Aleppo)
Al-Ladhiqiyah
Hamäh
Hims
Dayr az Zawr
Tudmur (Palmyra)

SYRIA
NORTH CYPRUS
Nicosia
CYPRUS
LEBANON
Beirut
Damascus (Dimashq)

IRAQ
SYRIAN
DESERT (BADIYAT ASH SHAM)

MEDITERRANEAN SEA

Tripoli (Tarābulus)
Al Khums
Misrātah
Zliṭan
Zāwiyah
afran
Qaṣr Banī Walīd
RĀBULUS (TRIPOLITANIA)
Ash Sharqīyah
Al Qaryah
Banghāzī
Zāwiyat al Bayḍā
Darnah
Al Marj
Ṭūkrah
Surt
Khalīj Surt
An Nawfalīyah
Ajdābiyah
Al-'Uqaylah
Qaṣr al Burayqah
BARQAH (CYRENAICA)
AL JABAL AL AKHDAR
Tubruq

Haifa
Tel Aviv-Yafo
ISRAEL
Jerusalem
Ghazzah
Port Said
Dumyāṭ
ALEXANDRIA (Al Iskandarīyah)
Sīdī Barrānī
Marsā Maṭrūḥ
As Sallūm
Al 'Alamayn
Damanhūr
Al Manṣūrah
Tanṭā
CAIRO (Al Qāhirah)
Az Zaqāzīq
Suez (As Suways)
Suez Canal
'Ammān
JORDAN
Al 'Aqabah
Al Jawf

Marādah
Awjilah
Wāḥat Jālū
Al Jaghbūb
Sīwah (Oasis)
MUNKHAFAD AL QATTĀRAH -436
LIBYAN
Bani Suwayf
Al Fayyūm
Birket Qārūn
Al Minyā
SINAI PEN.
Jabal Kātrīnā 868B
AN NAFŪD
Taymā'
Hā'il
Buraydah

Sawknah
Zillah
Zaltan
JABAL AS SAWDA
Al Jufrah (Oasis)
Tarbū
DESERT (AS SAHRĀ' AL LĪBĪYAH)
Qaṣr al Farāfirah
Al Bawīṭī
Asyūṭ
Akhmīm
Sawhāj
Būr Safājah
Al-Wajh
Al Quṣayr
ARABIAN DESERT
SAUDI
NAJD
ARABIA
Al Madīnah (Medina)

AZZĀN (FEZZAN)
Mārzuq
Tarbū
IDEHAN MARZŪQ
Buzaymah
Rebiana (Oasis)
Al Kufrah (Oasis)
Al Jawf
Qinā
Al Uqsur (Luxor)
Thebes (Ruins)
Idfū
Aswān High Dam
Aswān
RA'S BANĀS
AL ḤIJĀZ (HEJAZ)
Yanbu'

SARĪR TIBASTI
Ma'tan Bishārah
Bi'r Misāhah
Ash Shabb
Lake Nasser
ADMINISTRATIVE BOY.
Halā'ib
Jiddah
Mecca (Makkah)
Al Khurmah

Pic Touside 10 712
TIBESTI
Emi Koussi 11 204
Ounianga Kébir
Arbi
Kosha
Dalqū
NUBIAN DESERT
Jabal Erba 7 274
Bilma
BORKOU
BODELE
Largeau
Fada
ENNEDI
Yarda
Dunqulah
Al Khandaq
Kuraymah
Marawi
3rd Cataract
Abu Ḥamad
Būr Sūdān
Sawākin
Al Qunfudhah
Abhā
Qīzān
JAZĀ'IR FARASĀN
DAHLAK ARCH.
KAMARĀN

Agadem (Oasis)
Yao
Fada
Oum Chalouba
Al 'Aṭrūn
Ad Dabbah
Kūrtī
5th Cataract
Barbar
'Atbarah
Ad Dāmir
Adarama
Tawkar
Taqāṭu' Hayyā
Keren
Akordat
Mitsiwa (Massawa)
ERITREA
Asmera
Mersa Fatma
Al Ḥudaydah
YEMEN
Al Mukhā

Lake Chad (Lac Tchad)
Mao
CHAD
6th Cataract
Shandī
Omdurman (Umm Durmān)
Al Khartūm Bahrī
Khartoum (Al Khartūm)
Al Kāmilīn
Kassalā
Sebderat
Barentu
Adi Ugri
Adwa
Mekele
DENAKIL
Ed
N'Djamena (Fort-Lamy)
Abéché
DĀRFŪR
Al Fāshir
Jabal Marrah 10 131
SUDAN
KURDUFĀN
Al-Ubayyid
Ad Duwaym
Rufa 'ah
Wad Madani
Al Qaḍārif
Om Hajer
Ras Dashen Terara 15 158
Gonder
Sekota
Debre Tabor
Ras 'Ali
Aṣeb
MANDARA MTS.
Maroua
Bousso
Yao
Am Timan
An Nuhūd
Nyala
Al Uḍayyah
JIBĀL AN NUBAH
Kūstī
Sinjah
Sennar Dam
Sannār
Qallābāt
Dangila
Tala
Amba Farit 14 478
Dese
13 041
Werē Ilu
Tadjoura
DJIBOUTI
Djibouti
Aysha
Seylac
Léré
Laï
Bousso
Sarh
Talawdī
Malūṭ
Kurmuk
Asosa
Roseires Res.
Ar Ruṣayriṣ
Blue Nile (Abay)
Debre Markos
Dire Dawa
Harer
Chari
Bahr al Arab
An Nuhūd
Talawdī

CENTRAL AFRICAN REPUBLIC
Ngaoundéré
Koundé
Bouar
Fort-Sibut
Bambari
CHAÎNE DES MONGOS
Yalinga
Ndélé
Ouanda Djallé
Kafia Kingi
Lol
Bahr al Arab
AS SUDD
Malakāl
Kodok
Nāṣir
Nekemte
Tulu Welel 10 830
Dembi Dolo
Gore
Gambela
Jima
Shewa Gimira
ETHIOPIA
HARERGE
AHMAR MTS.
Goba
Ginir
SIDAMO

Bangui
Zongo
Mbaïki
Libenge
Gemena
Bangassou
Rafaï
Zémio
Gwane
Bondo
Bambesa
Dungu
Niangara
Watsa
Gombari
BAHR AL GHAZĀL
Shambe
Rumbek
Bor
Tambura
Mongalla
Jūbā
Kapoeta
Nimule
Chew Bahir (Lake Stefanie)
Maji
Chamo
Bako
Mega
Doolow
El Wak

DEMOCRATIC REPUBLIC OF THE CONGO
Yokadouma
Lomié
Ouesso
CONGO
Dongou
Impfondo
Makanza
Bomengo
Basankusu
Mbandaka
Lisala
Bumba
Bomongo
Basoko
Panga
Isangi
Kisangani (Stanleyville)
Boyoma Falls
Equator
Ake ti
Buta
Isiro
Niangara
Avakubi
Lindi
Mahagi Port
Arua
Irumu
L. Albert
Ft. Portal
Margherita Peak 16 763
UGANDA
Masindi
Soroti
Kitgum
KENYA
Mt. Elgon 14 178
Kampala
Entebbe
Jinja
Eldoret
Lake Victoria
Meru
SOMALIA
Moyale
Rabalega Falls

40,000 SQ MI AREA
0 100 200
Miles

0 50 100 200 300 400 500 Miles
0 100 200 400 600 800 Kilometers

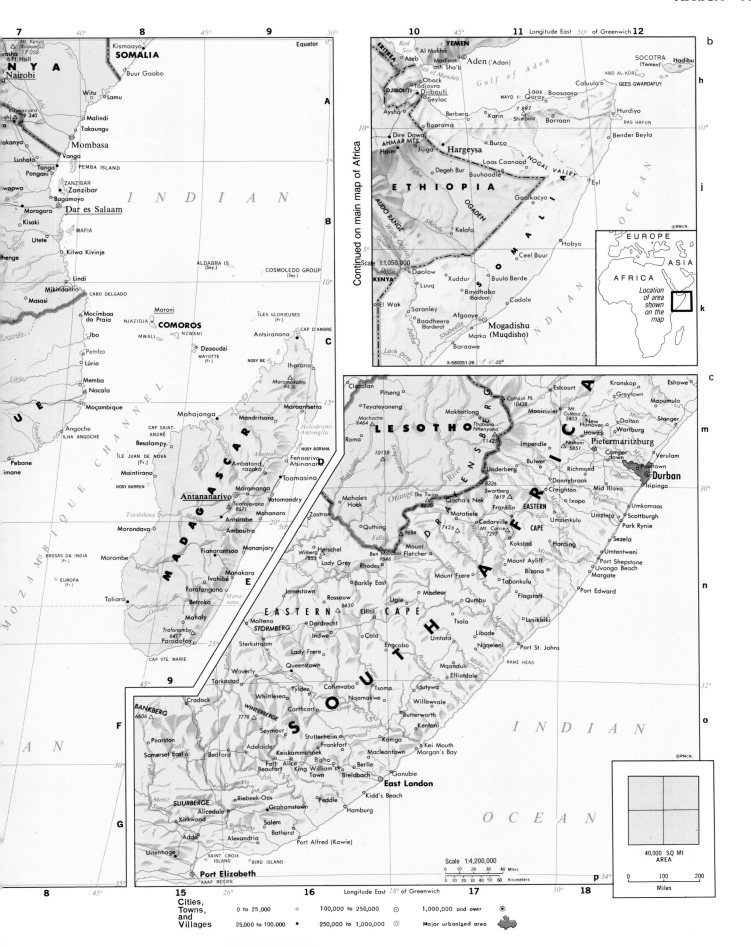

Cities,
Towns,
and
Villages

0 to 25,000   o   100,000 to 250,000   ⊙   1,000,000 and over   ⊙

25,000 to 100,000   •   250,000 to 1,000,000   ⊚   Major urbanized area

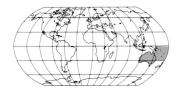

Oceania
Terrain

Deep in the heart of Australia, on the western plateau, lies Mount Olga. A worn-down collection of sandstone blocks, "the Olgas" and nearby Ayers Rock tower above the desert landscape.

A map of the world shows you just how big the Pacific Ocean is. It covers more than one-third of the earth's surface. You can also see that the ocean is full of islands of different sizes. Australia, New Zealand, and other islands in this region known as Oceania lie within the vast Pacific like stepping stones across a pond. Geographers group the islands into three regions. Polynesia includes Hawaii, Samoa, Tahiti, and Easter Island. Micronesia contains the Marshall, Caroline, and Gilbert islands. Melanesia includes the Fiji Islands and New Guinea.

Australia is the smallest continent. The Great Dividing Range thrusts its mountains along the eastern coast. In the south, it dips into the sea and rises up again to form Tasmania. Hammered by wind and water over hundreds of millions of years, the hump-shaped mountains of the Great Dividing Range are truly ancient.

West of the Great Dividing Range is the continent's great desert region. Australians call it the Outback. The mountains keep clouds and rain from moving into the Outback. Part of the Outback is bush country, where some trees and plants grow. The rest is made up of three deserts: the Great Sandy, the Gibson, and the Great Victoria.

The Cape York Peninsula is very different from the rest of Australia. Heat and rain combine to make ideal conditions for the tropical rain forests that grow there.

Perhaps the most famous region of Australia is not on the land, but in the ocean off the

northeastern coast. It is called the Great Barrier Reef. Built from colorful coral formations, it is the largest coral reef in the world and supports a great variety of ocean life.

Two main islands make up New Zealand: North Island and South Island. On the southwest coast of South Island, long, beautiful fjords cut into the land, just like the fjords of Norway. North Island boasts a volcanic region around Lake Taupo.

The Isle of Pines is one of several islands that make up New Caledonia. The culture and pleasant climate of this French territory attract many tourists.

Animals

Many of the animals of Australia are very different from those in other places. Australia was separated from all other parts of the world for about fifty million years, so its animals evolved in different ways, creating different solutions to the problems of survival. Most Australian *mammals*—furry, warm-blooded animals—are marsupials. Marsupials are animals like the kangaroo whose babies are kept in a pouch on the mother's body until they are old enough to care for themselves.

On the plains of Australia, several kinds of marsupials make their homes. Kangaroos live in little herds and eat grass. Some kangaroos can be as much as seven feet (over two meters) tall, but there are also small kangaroos called wallabies. Wombats look like beavers without tails. They dig tunnels that they sleep in during the day, and then forage for food at night. Ratlike, long-snouted bandicoots live much the same way as wombats.

Dingoes also roam the dry plains of Australia. When the first European settlers arrived, the dingo was the only large, meat-eating mammal on the continent. A member of the dog family, the dingo has long legs, a wolflike head, and yellow-red fur.

In the eastern part of Australia lives the koala. Koalas look like little bears, but in fact they are not. Unlike bears, which are mammals, koalas are marsupials and carry their young in pouches.

New Zealand does not have many animals that have not been brought by people. But on some islands near New Zealand live little reptiles called tuataras. They are the last survivors of a group of reptiles that lived about 225 million years ago—long before the rise of the dinosaurs.

Great numbers of sea creatures drift gracefully among the coral reefs and the deeper tropical waters surrounding the islands of Oceania. Most are brilliantly colored and very beautiful.

Blue Angelfish

Pacific Sheepshead

Albacore

Ocean Sunfish

Eagle Ray

Regal Angelfish

Imperial Angelfish

Sea Horse

Viperfish

Opah

Black Marlin

Triggerfish

Butterfly Fish

Cockatoo

Cassowary

Dingo

Death Adder

Tree Kangaroo

Echidna

Emu

Frilled Lizard

Rock Wallaby

Rabbit

Wombat

Great Gray Kangaroo

Koala

Kookaburra

Red Kangaroo

Platypus

Wandering Albatross

White Shark

Slender-billed Shearwater

Black Swan

The koala looks like a soft, cuddly teddy bear. Small, it weighs less than eighteen pounds (8.16 kilograms) when grown. For six months the cub rides in its mother's pouch. Later it rides on her back, even when she climbs high into the eucalyptus trees for the buds and leaves that are the koala's only food.

Dovey Petrel

Kiwi

Tuatara

Kea

OCEANIA
Life on the Land

- Lumbering
- Rain Forest
- Water Sports
- Sheep Raising
- Lumbering
- Uranium Prospecting
- Water Conservation
- Great Barrier Reef
- Mining
- Aborigines in the Outback
- Cattle Raising
- Agricultural Area
- Ayers Rock
- Sheep Raising
- Rugby
- Going to School by Radio
- Mining
- Opals Mined
- Sydney—Opera House
- Lifeguard Teams
- Minerals Mined
- Citrus Groves
- Agricultural Area
- Agricultural Area
- Wheatlands
- Water Sports
- Freighter
- Fishing
- Fruit Grown
- Minerals Exported

- Maori Carving
- Sheep Raising

During the Age of Discovery, Europeans traveled to Australia, New Zealand, and other islands of Oceania. They settled the lands they found, and many descendants of Europeans remain on those lands.

Australia may be the smallest continent, but it is also one of the largest countries. Its population clings mostly to the coasts along the fertile lands of the east and southeast. Some people live at the edge of the Outback. They are mostly farmers who raise sheep and cattle. Australia's major exports include grain and wool. Today, Australia is highly industrialized.

New Zealand is not as industrialized as Australia, but manufacturing areas such as the paper industry are growing. The mild climate and excellent grazing land makes the raising of sheep and cattle very important in New Zealand.

Countries and Cities

The Land Down Under— that's what Australia and New Zealand are often called. The nickname grew out of the idea that these lands are directly opposite, that is, under the feet of, Europeans.

Australia is divided into states, and its people elect their leaders. New Zealand, also once a British colony, now operates in much the same way.

The islands of Oceania were once colonies, too, but have become nations. Western Samoa, Nauru, Fiji, the Solomon Islands, and the eastern half of New Guinea are now independent.

The descendants of Europeans who live in Australia and New Zealand speak English. There are groups of people in these places and on the surrounding islands who have lived there since ancient times, and most of them speak English, as well as the languages of their ancestors.

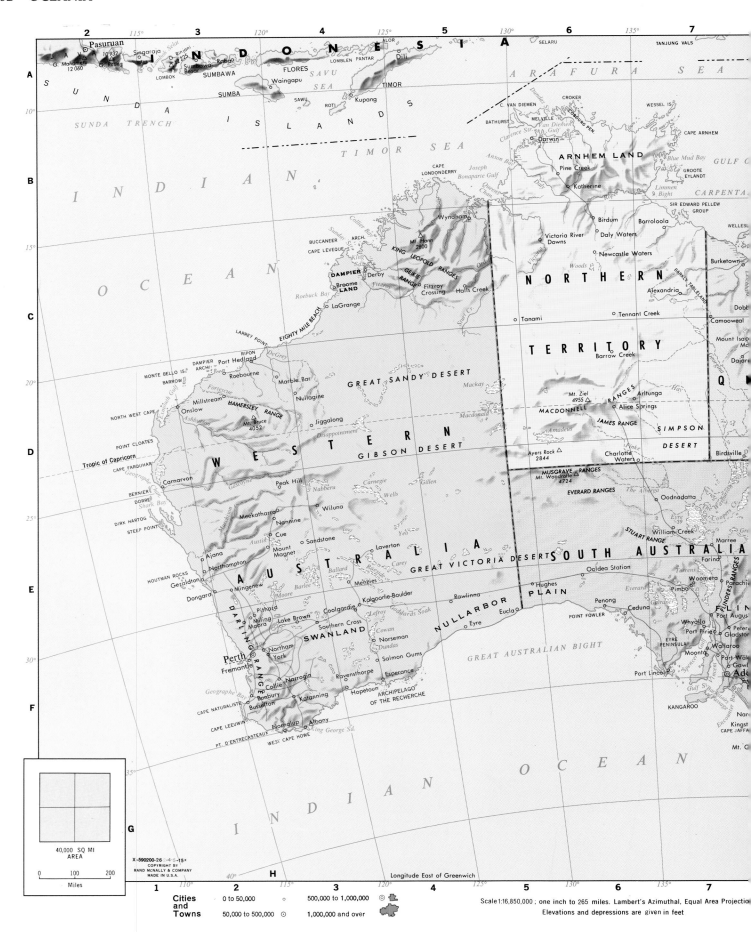

40,000 SQ MI
AREA

0   100   200
Miles

Cities
and
Towns

o	0 to 50,000
⊙	50,000 to 500,000
◎	500,000 to 1,000,000
	1,000,000 and over

Longitude East of Greenwich

Scale 1:16,850,000 ; one inch to 265 miles. Lambert's Azimuthal, Equal Area Projection
Elevations and depressions are given in feet

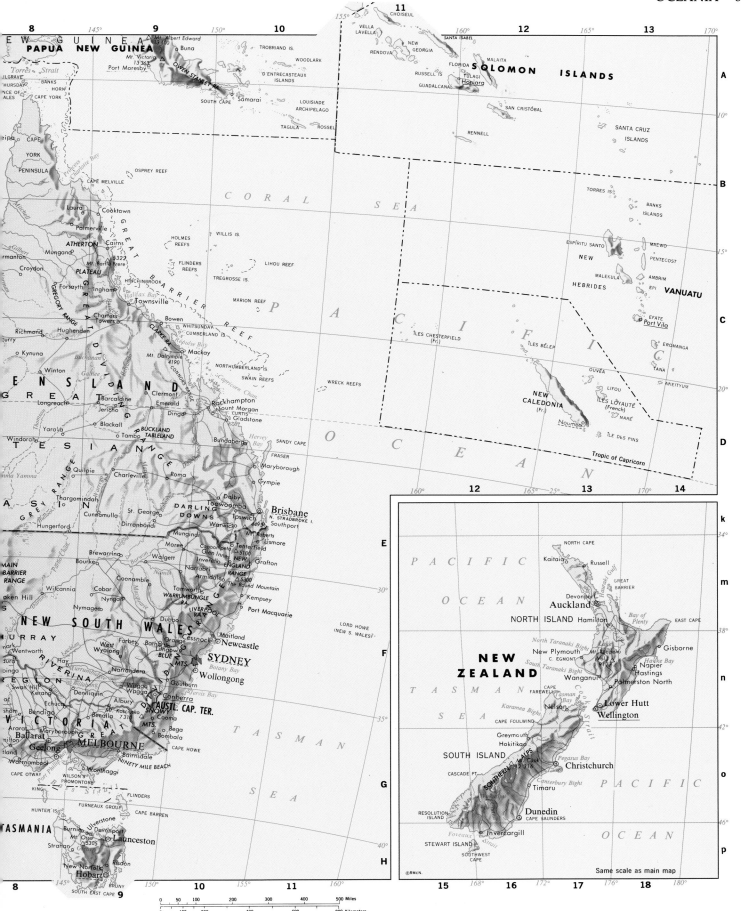

PAPUA NEW GUINEA

NEW GUINEA
Mt. Albert Edward 13,100
Mt. Victoria 13,363
Buna
Port Moresby
OWEN STANLEY RA.
SOUTH CAPE
Samarai
D'ENTRECASTEAUX ISLANDS
TROBRIAND IS.
WOODLARK
LOUISIADE ARCHIPELAGO
Tagula   Rossel

Torres Strait
JLGRAVE
THURSDAY
NCE OF ALES
HORN
CAPE YORK
BANKS
CAPE YORK PENINSULA
Princess Charlotte Bay
CAPE MELVILLE

SOLOMON ISLANDS

CHOISEUL
VELLA LAVELLA
RENDOVA
NEW GEORGIA
SANTA ISABEL
MALAITA
FLORIDA
RUSSELL IS.
TULAGI
GUADALCANAL   Honiara
SAN CRISTÓBAL
RENNELL
SANTA CRUZ ISLANDS

CORAL   SEA

OSPREY REEF

TORRES IS.
BANKS ISLANDS

CAPE
YORK
Laura
Cooktown
Palmerville
ATHERTON   Cairns
Mungand
PLATEAU
Forsayth
Ingham
Mt. Bartle Frere 5322
Croydon
manton
Gilbert
HINCHINBROOK I.
Townsville
Charters Towers
Bowen
WHITSUNDAY
CUMBERLAND IS.
Repulse Bay
Mackay
Mt. Dalrymple 4190
NORTHUMBERLAND IS.
SWAIN REEFS
WRECK REEFS

HOLMES REEFS
WILLIS IS.
FLINDERS REEFS
TREGROSSE IS.
MARION REEF
LIHOU REEF

GREAT   BARRIER   REEF
Halifax Bay

ESPÍRITU SANTO
NEW HEBRIDES
MALEKULA
MAEWO
PENTECOST
AMBRIM
EPI   VANUATU
AMBRIM
EFATE   Port Vila

Richmond
Kynuna
Winton
Hughenden
curry
DIVIDING
CLARKE RA.

ÎLES CHESTERFIELD (Fr.)
ÎLES BÉLEP
EROMANGA

PACIFIC

Longreach
Barcaldine
Jericho
Clermont
Emerald
Dingo
Rockhampton
Mount Morgan
CURTIS
Gladstone
Yarala
Blackall
Tambo
BUCKLAND TABLELAND
Bundaberg
Hervey Bay
SANDY CAPE
CONNORS RANGE
Capricorn Chan.

QUEENSLAND
GREAT
Buchanan
Galilee
Thomson
Barcoo

NEW CALEDONIA (Fr.)
Nouméa
ÎLE DES PINS
ÎLES LOYAUTÉ (French)
MARÉ
OUVÉA
LIFOU
TANA
ANEITYUM

Windorah
ma Yamma
Quilpie
Charleville
Roma
Maryborough
FRASER
Bulloo
Warrego

TES I A N   RANGE
GREAT   ARTESIAN   BASIN

Thargomindah
Cunnamulla
Hungerford
St. George
Dirranbandi
DARLING DOWNS
Dalby
Toowoomba
Warwick
Ipswich
Brisbane
N. STRADBROKE I.
Southport
Gympie

OCEAN

Tropic of Capricorn

Mungindi
Moree
Mt. Roberts
Lismore
Tenterfield 5100
Glen Innes
Inverell
NEW ENGLAND RANGE
Grafton
The Round Mountain 5300
Capoompeta

Brewarrina
Bourke
Walgett
Narrabri
Armidale
Kempsey

MAIN BARRIER RANGE
Wilcannia
Cobar
Coonamble
Nyngan
Tamworth
WARRUMBUNGLE RA.
LIVERPOOL RA.
Port Macquarie

Broken Hill
Nymagee
Dubbo
Nyngan

NEW SOUTH WALES

Orange
Cessnock
Maitland
Newcastle

Forbes
West Wyalong
Bathurst
Lithgow
BLUE MTS.
SYDNEY
Botany Bay
Wollongong

MURRAY
Hay
Narrandera
Wagga Wagga
Canberra
Jervis Bay
AUSTL. CAP. TER.

RIVERINA
Deniliquin
Kerang
Albury
Mt. Kosciusko 7316
SNOWY MTS.
Cooma
Goulburn

REGION
Wentworth
Echuca
Bendigo
Benalla
Bombala
Bega
Bairnsdale
CAPE HOWE

VICTORIA

Ararat
Maryborough
GREAT
Ballarat
Geelong
MELBOURNE
Warrnambool
CAPE OTWY
Port Phillip
Wonthaggi
NINETY MILE BEACH
WILSON'S PROMONTORY

TASMAN

SEA

KING
FLINDERS
FURNEAUX GROUP
CAPE BARREN
HUNTER IS.

TASMANIA

Burnie
Ulverstone
Devonport
Mt. Ossa 5305
Strahan
New Norfolk
Hobart
Launceston
BRUNY
SOUTH EAST CAPE

NEW ZEALAND

PACIFIC   OCEAN

NORTH CAPE
Kaitaia
Russell
GREAT BARRIER
Devonport
Auckland
Hamilton
Huraki Gulf
Bay of Plenty
EAST CAPE

NORTH ISLAND

North Taranaki Bight
New Plymouth
C. EGMONT
Mt. Egmont
South Taranaki Bight
Wanganui
Gisborne
Hawke Bay
Napier
Hastings
Palmerston North

TASMAN
CAPE FAREWELL
Karamea Bight
Nelson
Tasman Bay
Lower Hutt
Wellington
Cook Strait

SEA
CAPE FOULWIND
Greymouth
Hokitika

SOUTH ISLAND

SOUTHERN ALPS
Mt. Cook 12,349
Pegasus Bay
Christchurch
Canterbury Bight
Timaru

PACIFIC

CASCADE PT.
RESOLUTION ISLAND
Dunedin
CAPE SAUNDERS

Foveaux Strait
Invercargill
STEWART ISLAND
SOUTHWEST CAPE

OCEAN

©RMcN.

Same scale as main map

0   50   100   200   300   400   500 Miles
0   100   200   400   600   800 Kilometers

North America
Terrain

North America

Third largest continent

•

Fourth in population: 464,800,000

•

28 cities with over 2 million population

•

Highest mountain: McKinley, 20,320 feet (6,194 meters)

•

World's largest island: Greenland

•

Location of North Magnetic Pole

North America has several mountainous areas. The western mountains are made up of two main chains that stretch from Alaska at the northern end of the continent to Panama at the southern end. The Rocky Mountains rise out of the Great Plains. The Rockies reach into Canada,

where they are even more spectacular than they are in the United States.

The Great Basin lies between the two western mountain chains in the United States. Mountains prevent most of the Pacific moisture from reaching the Great Basin,

Coral reefs and submarine volcanoes formed the islands of the Caribbean. Many of the coral islands are flat and low-lying, while those of volcanic origin tend to be rugged. Shown here is volcanic Saba in the Leeward Islands.

© 1979 Rand McNally & Co.

British Columbia is the westernmost province of Canada. Its mountainous terrain once isolated it from the rest of the country. Today it is the site of several national parks, including Yoho National Park, shown here.

Monument Valley lies on the border between Utah and Arizona. Here sandstone buttes, mesas, and arches rise above the sandy plain below—some as high as one thousand feet (three hundred meters).

and the southern end of the basin is a desert. Farther south, a desertlike region covers much of the American Southwest and reaches deep into Mexico.

The two mountain chains extend into Mexico as well. The Sierra Madre Occidental is in the west, and the Sierra Madre Oriental is in the east. Plateau country spreads out between them, and it is here that most Mexicans live. Central America, at the south end of North America, is mainly mountainous.

The mountains of eastern North America are much lower than the ones to the west. Some of them are older mountains, and they have been worn down by time and weather. One such range is the Appalachians, the biggest mountain range in the eastern United States.

The Great Plains lie at the center of North America. This region is one of the largest plains on Earth, and the land is mostly flat or gently rolling as far as the eye can see.

North America has several important rivers and bodies of water. The Mississippi and Missouri rivers form the longest river system on the continent. Lake Superior, one of the five Great Lakes, is the largest freshwater lake in the world. The Panama Canal, near the southern tip of North America, is a human-made strip of water that allows ships to pass between the Atlantic and the Pacific oceans without having to go all the way around the southern tip of South America.

NORTH AMERICA
Animals

As the number of people in North America has increased, the number of wild animals has decreased. People have hunted some animals to extinction.

The buffalo, or American bison, was once nearly wiped out by hunters. The pronghorn antelope had a similar fate. Conservation efforts kept both species from extinction, and today they are found in protected areas on the Great Plains.

Wolves and mighty grizzly bears prowl in the north. The bald eagle, the national bird of the United States, is still found in the Northwest. These animals are endangered today.

The coyote, a symbol of the American West, preys on prairie dogs, mice, rabbits, and sometimes on livestock. Raccoons can be found from southern Canada to South America, except in parts of the Rockies and in deserts. Looking like a masked bandit, the raccoon forages at night and will feed on garbage. Both animals seem to thrive near people.

Many kinds of rattlesnakes, named for the rattles on their tails, inhabit North America. The largest of them is the eastern diamondback, often seven feet (over two meters) long. The coral snake, a colorful relative of the cobra, also lives in the deserts, as does a poisonous lizard called the Gila monster.

In the swamps and rivers of the southeastern part of the continent lives the alligator. These meat-eating reptiles can reach nine feet (2.7 meters) in length. Hunted for their skins, alligators are now protected.

It has been said that most of the animals that have ever lived on earth are now extinct. We know about prehistoric animals only from their fossil remains. Extinctions still occur, some of them the result of human interference. The passenger pigeon was seen and painted by John James Audubon in 1840.

Apatosaurus
135 Million Years Ago

Tyrannosaurus
70 Million Years Ago

Woolly Mammoth
10 Thousand Years Ago

Great Auk
Mid Nineteenth Century

Saber-Toothed Cat
1 Million Years Ago

Passenger Pigeon
Late Nineteenth Century

Grizzly Bear

Walrus

Herring Gull

Canada Goose

Polar Bear

Mountain Goat

Red Fox

Gray Wolf

Rock Ptarmigan

Bald Eagle

Beaver

Porcupine

Mountain Lion

Moose

King Salmon

Pronghorn

Robin

Elk

Gray Squirrel

Sea Otter

Raccoon

White-tailed Deer

Willet

Bison

Cottontail

Gambel's Quail

California Sea Lions

Diamondback Rattlesnake

Opossum

Turkey

Peccary

Alligator

Armadillo

Roseate Spoonbill

Brown Pelican

Squirrel Monkey

Gray Whale

NORTH AMERICA
Life on the Land

Ice hockey is a popular sport played by both amateurs and professionals in Canada and the United States, as well as in other countries. Hockey is the national sport of Canada.

The United States and Canada, two of the three largest countries in North America, are also among the richest nations in the world. Many factors contribute to this abundant wealth, including agriculture. North America has much fertile farmland and a good climate for growing a variety of crops.

Rich mineral deposits also contribute to the prosperity of the United States and Canada. Mineral exports from these countries include copper, lead, asbestos, zinc, silver, nickel, coal, crude oil, and natural gas.

North America's rich forests and mineral reserves have helped the United States and Canada to become world leaders in manufacturing. Many cities in these countries have been huge industrial centers for many years, but this is gradually changing.

Agriculture is very important in Mexico and in other countries of North America as well. Corn is grown in Mexico. In Central America and the islands called the West Indies, coffee, sugarcane, and bananas are grown. But much of the land in these countries is not good for growing crops, and many of the farmers do not have modern machinery.

There is not as much manufacturing in the other countries of North America, although the iron, steel, and chemical industries are growing. Mexico is also a leading producer of silver and petroleum. Tourists, interested in the country's sunny climate and ancient ruins, also help the economy.

According to folklore, the giant Paul Bunyan and his enormous blue ox Babe created much of America's landscape. The legend claims that they dug the St. Lawrence River in three weeks using a shovel as large as a house.

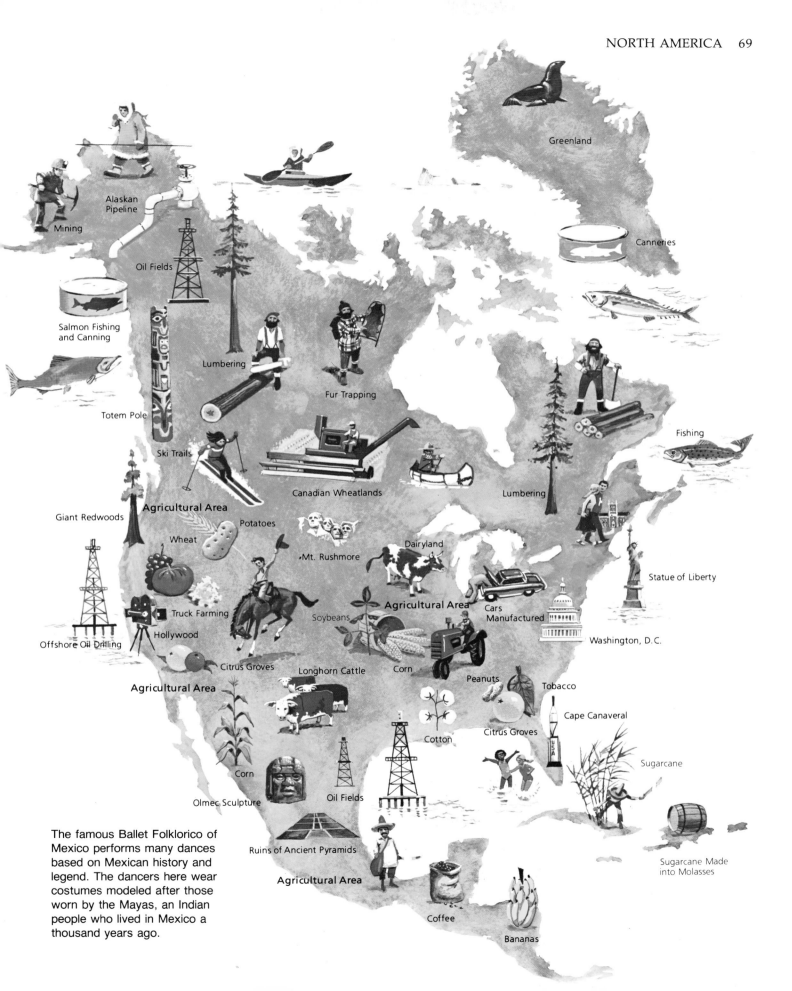

Greenland

Mining
Alaskan Pipeline
Oil Fields
Salmon Fishing and Canning
Totem Pole
Lumbering
Fur Trapping
Canneries
Ski Trails
Canadian Wheatlands
Lumbering
Fishing
Agricultural Area
Giant Redwoods
Wheat
Potatoes
Mt. Rushmore
Dairyland
Statue of Liberty
Truck Farming
Soybeans
Agricultural Area
Cars Manufactured
Washington, D.C.
Offshore Oil Drilling
Hollywood
Citrus Groves
Longhorn Cattle
Corn
Peanuts
Tobacco
Agricultural Area
Cape Canaveral
Corn
Cotton
Citrus Groves
Olmec Sculpture
Oil Fields
Sugarcane
Ruins of Ancient Pyramids
Agricultural Area
Sugarcane Made into Molasses
Coffee
Bananas

The famous Ballet Folklorico of Mexico performs many dances based on Mexican history and legend. The dancers here wear costumes modeled after those worn by the Mayas, an Indian people who lived in Mexico a thousand years ago.

NORTH AMERICA
Countries and Cities

Mexico City is the capital and fastest-growing city of that nation. It is among the five most populous cities of the world. In 1985, the city suffered a major earthquake, which caused much damage and killed thousands.

O f all the continents, the boundaries between countries are the simplest in North America. Most of the continent is divided among three nations: Canada, the United States, and Mexico. Central America, considered a part of North America, covers an area less than a third the size of Mexico and contains seven countries.

The countries of North America are mainly inhabited by descendants of Europeans who crossed the seas after the 1500s. Native Americans, the people who lived here long before the Europeans arrived, still populate some areas and many live close to the way their ancestors lived.

Like the people of the conti-nent's three largest nations, most North Americans elect their leaders. In some coun-tries, such as Panama, military leaders have taken control of the government. For Panama, at least, this may now be changing. Cuba, an island na-tion in the Caribbean, has long had a communist government.

The main language of each North American nation is the language spoken in the Euro-pean country that once domi-nated the area. For example, Spain once ruled Mexico, and although Mexico is now inde-pendent, its people still speak Spanish.

Cities usually grow up around areas that are accessi-ble to trade routes, and the cit-ies of North America are no exception. Many of them sprung up near bodies of water that were traveled by the many traders who ex-plored the land. For example, Chicago, Illinois, grew up on a

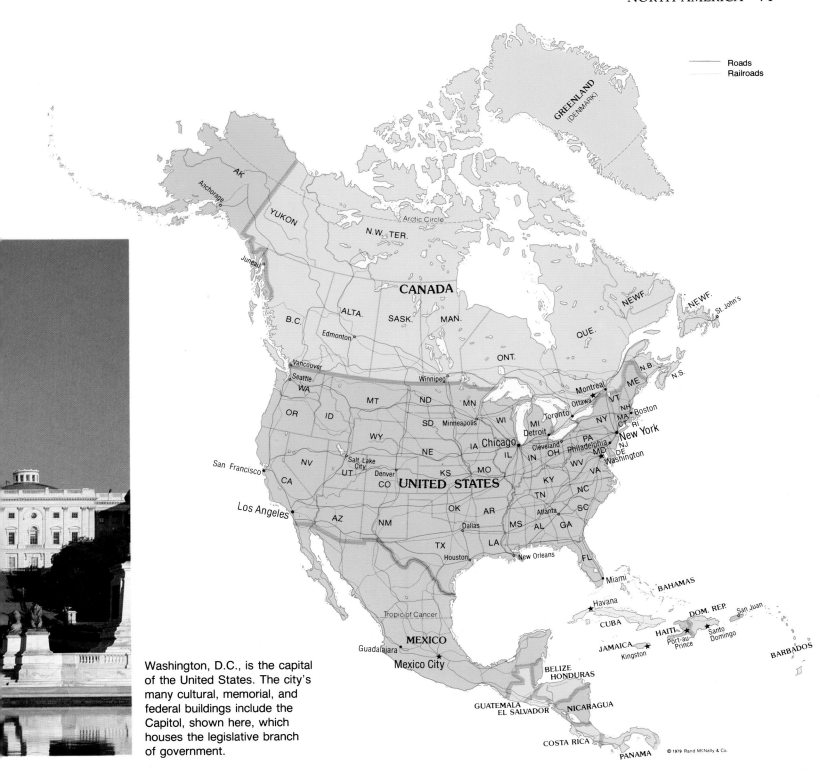

Roads
Railroads

Washington, D.C., is the capital of the United States. The city's many cultural, memorial, and federal buildings include the Capitol, shown here, which houses the legislative branch of government.

crossroads that linked the Great Lakes and the Mississippi River. Detroit, Toronto, Ottawa, and Cleveland have a similar history.

Today, some of the biggest and most modern cities in the world are in North America. The population of New York City is one of the largest in the world. With over 8.8 million people, Mexico City is even larger. In fact, Mexico is the most populous Spanish-speaking country in the world and carries much influence with those nations.

Scale 1:12,600,000; one inch to 200 miles. Conic Projection
Elevations and depressions are given in feet

Cities, Towns, and Villages

0 to 25,000 ○   100,000 to 250,000 ◉   1,000,000 and over ◉

25,000 to 100,000 •   250,000 to 1,000,000 ◎   Major urbanized area

Longitude West of Greenwich

Same scale as main map

QUEBEC

CAPE BAULD

Strait of Belle Isle

Gulf of

St. Lawrence

LONG RANGE MTS.

GROS MORNE
NAT'L PARK
Deer Lake

Corner Brook

Stephenville

C. ST. GEORGE

St. George's Bay

NEWFOUNDLAND

St. George's

Botwood

Grand Falls

Windsor

Gander

Notre Dame Bay

White Bay

Twillingate

Bonavista

TERRA NOVA
NAT'L PARK

Red Indian

Trinity

Bonavista Bay

Trinity Bay

CAPE RAY

Channel-Port-aux-Basques

Cabot Strait

CAPE NORTH

Grand Bank

Burin

Fortune Bay

St. John's

Placentia Bay

CAPE BRETON
ISLAND

ST. PIERRE AND MIQUELON (Fr.)

ATLANTIC OCEAN

© RMcN

BAFFIN
ISLAND
NAT'L PARK

Igloolik

Foxe
Basin

MELVILLE
PENINSULA

Arctic Circle

PRINCE
CHARLES
ISLAND

BAFFIN

ISLAND

Pangnirtung

Nettilling

CUMBERLAND
PEN.

Cumberland Sound

C. DE MERCY

Iqaluit

Amadjuak

Frobisher Bay

HALL
PEN.

Lake Harbour

EVERETT
MTS.

RESOLUTION

SOUTHAMPTON
ISLAND

BELL
PEN.

Roes Welcome Sound

Fisher Strait

C. LOW

MANSEL

COATS

NOTTINGHAM
ISLAND

SALISBURY

Hudson

FOXE
PEN.

FOXE
CHANNEL

Foxe
Channel

Ivujivik

C. DE
NOUVELLE-
FRANCE

C. HOPES
ADVANCE

AKPATOK

KILLING I.

TORNGAT
MTS.

Hebron

Nain

Strait

PENINSULE

D'UNGAVA

Payne

aux Feuilles

Kuujjuaq

Ungava
Bay

Povungnituk

OTTAWA
ISLANDS

Minto

Koksoak

Kaniapiscau

NEW

FOUND

Hopedale

Makkovik

Rigolet

Hamilton Inlet

Cartwright

HUDSON

BAY

All islands within bays and straits
lie within Northwest Territories.

Grande de la Baleine

BELCHER
ISLANDS

Ft. Severn

Severn

Winisk

C. HENRIETTA MARIA

PTE. LOUIS-XIV

La Grande

Chisasibi

Nichicun

James
Bay

Akimiski

Lac
Bienville

Opinaca

Eastmain

Caniapiscau

Ashuanipi

Schefferville

Naskaupi

Michikamau

Happy
Valley-
Goose Bay

Churchill Falls

Goose Bay

Little Mecatina

MEALY MTS.

LABRADOR

LONG RANGE MTS.

Battle Harbour

C. ST. ANTHONY

Sault au Cochon

GROS MORNE
NAT'L PARK

Corner Brook

Stephenville

St. George's

Ft. Albany

Moosonee

Ft. Severn

R. de Rupert

Nottaway

Mistassini

Chibougamau

MTS.
OTISH

Peribonka

R aux Outardes

Manicouagan

Lac
Manicouagan

Minégan

ILE D'ANTICOSTI

Romaine

Natashquan

Natashquan

QUEBEC

Coral Rapids

Fraserdale

ONTARIO

Kapuskasing

Cochrane

Iroquois Falls

Timmins

Kirkland Lake

Ft. Albany

Missinaibi

Coral Rapids

Chapleau

Matagami

Waswanipi

Dolbeau

St. Félicien
Roberval
Chambord

Alma

Kenogami

Chicoutimi

Jonquière

Lac
St-Jean

Saguenay

St. Lawrence River

Rimouski

Matane

Cap-Chat

CHIC-CHOCS
MTS.

Mont-Joli

Rivière-du-Loup

Edmundston

PEN. DE GASPÉ

Gaspé

Chandler

New Carlisle

New Richmond

Caraquet

Chaleur Bay

Chatham

Bathurst

Newcastle

Richibucto

NEW

BRUNSWICK

Moncton

ILES DE LA
MADELEINE

Gulf of

St. Lawrence

Sept-Îles

Clarke City

Baie-Comeau

Betsiamites

PRINCE EDWARD
NAT'L PARK

Summerside

Charlottetown

P.E.I.

Amherst

Springhill

Truro

New
Glasgow

Sydney Mines

Sydney

CAPE BRETON
HIGHLANDS
NAT'L PARK

CANADA
U.S.A.

La Sarre

Amos

Senneterre

Rouyn

Malartic

Val-d'Or

Ville-Marie

Cobalt

Témiscaming

Parent

Réservoir Gouin

La Tuque

St-Maurice

Shawinigan

Trois-
Rivières

Grand'
Mère

Québec

Lévis

Victoriaville

Drummondville

Granby

Woodstock

Lac-
Frontière

MAINE

Fredericton

FUNDY
NAT'L PARK

Saint John

Sussex

St. George

St. Stephen

St. Andrews

Digby

Bay
of
Fundy

Kentville

Windsor

NOVA SCOTIA

Halifax

Dartmouth

Greenwood

Bridgewater

Liverpool

Shelburne

Yarmouth

CAPE SABLE

Sherbrooke

VERMONT

NEW HAMPSHIRE

Augusta

Concord

Portland

BOSTON

CAPE COD

ATLANTIC

OCEAN

Chapleau

Sudbury

North
Bay

Sturgeon Falls

Mattawa

Ottawa

Pembroke

Renfrew

Huntsville

Bancroft

Smiths Falls

Brockville

Kingston

Ogdensburg

Alexandria
Bay

MICHIPICOTEN I.

PUKASKWA
NAT'L PARK

Thunder Bay

Lake Superior

Marathon

Nipigon

Terrace Bay

Marquette

Sault Ste. Marie

Thessalon

Blind River

Espanola

MANITOULIN

Georgian
Bay

Parry Sound

Wiarton

Midland

Barrie

Orillia

Peterborough

Lindsay

Cobourg

Trenton

Lake Ontario

Rochester

Syracuse

NEW YORK

Albany

Hartford

MASS.

CONN.

Providence

R.I.

Escanaba

Sault Ste. Marie

WISCONSIN

Green Bay

MICHIGAN

Owen Sound

Kincardine

Saginaw

Flint

Lansing

Grand
Rapids

Sarnia

Port
Huron

DETROIT

Windsor

Leamington

Chatham

London

St. Thomas

St.
Catharines

Hamilton

TORONTO

Kitchener

Whitby

Oshawa

Niagara
Falls

BUFFALO

NEW YORK

Scranton

PENNSYLVANIA

New York

N.J.

Duluth

Superior

St. Paul

MINNEAPOLIS

Madison

MILWAUKEE

CHICAGO

ILLINOIS

Toledo

OHIO

Lake Michigan

Lake Huron

Lake Erie

Mississippi

Nipigon

Longlac

Geraldton

Nakina

Hearst

Armstrong Sta.

Sioux Lookout

Dryden

Red Lake

Lake of the Woods

Rainy

Lac Seul

St. Joseph

Trout

Winnipeg

X-520200-26   -9-8-27
COPYRIGHT BY
RAND McNALLY & COMPANY
MADE IN U.S.A.

40,000 SQ MI
AREA

0   100   200

Miles

0 25 50 75 100   200   300   400   500 Miles

0   100   200   400   600   800 Kilometers

Scale 1:12,600,000; one inch to 200 miles. Polyconic Projection
Elevations and depressions are given in feet

Cities
and
Towns

| 0 to 50,000 | 500,000 to 1,000,000 |
| 50,000 to 500,000 | 1,000,000 and over |

12

40,000 SQ MI
AREA

0   100   200

Miles

0 25 50 75 100   200   300   400   500 Miles

0   100   200   400   600   800 Kilometers

PANAMA

Scale 1:1,080,000

Scale 1:17,200,000; one inch to 270 miles. Polyconic Projection
Elevations and depressions are given in feet

X-530000-26 -10 26
COPYRIGHT BY
RAND MCNALLY & COMPANY
MADE IN U.S.A.

Puerto Rico inset (Scale 1:4,300,000)

ATLANTIC OCEAN

Aguadilla • Arecibo • San Juan • Bayamón • CABEZAS DE SAN JUAN • ST. THOMAS (U.S.A.) • TORTOLA (Br.)

PTA. HIGUERO • Utuado • Fajardo • CULEBRA • Charlotte Amalie (U.S.A.) • ST. JOHN (U.S.A.)

PUERTO RICO (U.S.A.)

Mayagüez • Caguas • Humacao • Vieques • VIEQUES

CABO ROJO • Coamo • Cayey

Ponce • Salinas • Guayama • Christiansted

CARIBBEAN SEA • SAINT CROIX (U.S.A.)

Scale 1:4,300,000
0 10 20 30 40 Miles
0 10 20 30 40 50 60 Kilometers
©RMcN.

St. Thomas inset (Scale 1:5,400,000)

LITTLE HANS LOLLICK
OUTER BRASS • HANS LOLLICK
INNER BRASS • PICARA PT • GRASS CAY
STORMY PT • THATCH CAY
ST. △ THOMAS (U.S.A.)
Crown Mt. 1558
Charlotte Amalie (St. Thomas) • Nadir
WATER
FLAMINGO PT • St. Thomas Harbor
©RMcN.
Scale 1:5,400,000

Main map

W. VIRGINIA • Richmond • Roanoke
VIRGINIA • Norfolk • Chesapeake Bay
Raleigh • CAPE HATTERAS
NORTH CAROLINA • Charlotte
Mt. Mitchell 6684
SOUTH CAROLINA • Wilmington • CAPE FEAR
Columbia • Charleston
Augusta
GEORGIA • Savannah

BERMUDA (Br.)

Tallahassee • Jacksonville
St. Augustine
Ocala
FLORIDA • CAPE CANAVERAL
Tampa
Tampa Bay

W. Palm Beach
Lake Okeechobee
GRAND BAHAMA • GREAT ABACO
CAPE SABLE
MIAMI
Key West • FLORIDA KEYS
Straits of Florida
ANDROS • Nassau • ELEUTHERA
CAT
SAN SALVADOR (WATLING)
LONG

HAVANA • Guanabacoa • Matanzas
Marianao • Cárdenas
Santa Clara
Pinar del Río • Sancti Spíritus
Cienfuegos • Ciego de Ávila
Trinidad • Camagüey • Nuevitas
ISLA DE LA JUVENTUD
Manzanillo • Holguín
SIERRA MAESTRA • Guantánamo
PUNTA MAISI
Santiago de Cuba
C. CRUZ
GRAND CAYMAN (Br.)

ACKLINS
CAICOS (Br.) • TURKS (Br.)
GT. INAGUA

PUERTO RICO TRENCH

NORTH AMERICAN BASIN

Cap-Haïtien • Puerto Plata • Santiago de los Caballeros • C. SAMANA
∇ 28 374
Gonaïves • Sánchez
ÎLE DE LA GONAVE • HAITI • DOMINICAN REPUBLIC • C. ENGAÑO
Pico Duarte 3417
Port-au-Prince • Santo Domingo
HISPANIOLA
Mayagüez • San Juan
Ponce • Charlotte Amalie
PUERTO RICO (U.S.A.)
VIRGIN IS. (ST. THOMAS)
ANGUILLA (Br.)
BARBUDA
SAINT CROIX (U.S.A.)
ST. KITTS AND NEVIS • ANTIGUA AND BARBUDA
MONTSERRAT (Br.)
V. Soufrière 4813 • Pointe-à-Pitre
Basse-Terre • GUADELOUPE (Fr.)
DOMINICA
MARTINIQUE (Fr.)
Fort-de-France
ST. LUCIA
ST. VINCENT AND THE GRENADINES • BARBADOS
Kingstown • Bridgetown
GRENADA

Montego Bay • Mt. Denham 2236 • Port Antonio
Spanish Town • JAMAICA • Kingston

WEST INDIES
ANTILLES
LESSER ANTILLES
WINDWARD IS.
WINDWARD PASSAGE
Mona Passage

TOBAGO
PUNTA DE GALLINAS • ARUBA (Neth.) • SAN ROMAN • CURAÇAO (Neth.) • BONAIRE (Neth.)
PENÍNSULA DE GUAJIRA • PEN. DE PARAGUANÁ • Willemstad
Santa Marta • Ciénaga • Coro • ISLA LA TORTUGA • ISLA DE MARGARITA
Barranquilla • Soledad • San Felipe • Puerto Cabello • CARACAS • Cumaná • TRINIDAD AND TOBAGO
Cartagena • Golfo del Venezuela • Maracaibo • Cabimas • La Guaira • Maracay • Puerto la Cruz • Carúpano • Port of Spain
Bluefields • Lorica • Sincelejo • Mompós • Barquisimeto • Valencia • Maturín • TRINIDAD
AMERICA • Golfo de los Mosquitos • Colón • DE PANAMA • Golfo del Darién • Magangué • Lago de Maracaibo • Trujillo • Guanare • Calabozo • El Tigre • Morawhanna
n José • Limón • Portobelo • Monteria • Valera • Mérida • Puerto de Nutrias • San Fernando de Apure • Ciudad Guayana
RICA • Cartago • ISTMO • Panamá • PANAMÁ • Ocaña • Cerro Bolívar • Ciudad Bolívar
David • Santiago • Antón • PEN. DE AZUERO • Golfo de Panamá • Pamplona • Bucaramanga • Cúcuta • San Cristóbal • VENEZUELA • Rio Orinoco
COIBA • Barrancabermeja • Cerro Icutu 7800 △
Medellín • Sonsón • Tunja • Salto Angel
Manizales • BOGOTÁ • GUYANA
Pereira • Armenia • COLOMBIA
ISLA DE MALPELO (Colombia) • Ibagué • Girardot • Villavicencio • San Fernando de Atabapo
Buenaventura • Cali • Palmira • SERRA PACARAIMA
Guaviare • Rio Orinoco • Ventuari
BRAZIL

Longitude West of Greenwich

0 50 100 200 300 400 500 Miles
0 100 200 400 600 800 Kilometers

Cities and Towns
0 to 50,000 ○
50,000 to 500,000 ⊙
500,000 to 1,000,000 ◎
1,000,000 and over

40 000 SQ MI AREA
0 100 200 Miles

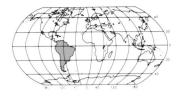

South America

Fourth largest continent

•

Fifth in population: 330,900,000

•

15 cities with over 2 million population

•

Highest mountain: Aconcagua,
22,831 feet (6,959 meters)

•

World's highest waterfall: Angel Falls,
3,212 feet (979 meters)

•

Equator passes through

The Sierra of Peru is a high-altitude region of gentle slopes surrounded by the towering peaks of the Andes. Farmland is found between the mountains; this is a farming community near the Urubamba River.

South America
Terrain

Kaieteur National Park in central Guyana lies in a region of forested highlands and plateaus. Wind and water have molded the park's sandstone and shale into a variety of interesting formations.

The Andes Mountains run down the entire western side of South America. Stretching more than four thousand miles (about 6,500 kilometers), the Andes chain is the longest in the world. This range also has some of the world's tallest peaks. Only the Himalayas in Asia are higher than Argentina's Mount Aconcagua.

Where Argentina, Bolivia, and Chile meet, the Andes split into two ranges. They are separated by a plateau about four hundred miles (about 650 kilometers) wide. This is called the Altiplano, or high plateau.

In northern Chile, between the Andes and the Pacific, is the Atacama Desert. This de-sert is near the ocean, yet it is one of the driest spots on earth. In some parts of the Atacama, no rainfall has ever been recorded.

Many rivers and streams tumble from the Andes and other highland areas. The Amazon River begins in the Andes of Peru and flows almost four thousand miles (more than six thousand kilometers) to the Atlantic Ocean. The Amazon contains more water than any other river on earth. Over four million cubic feet (more than 113,000 cubic meters) pour out of the Amazon and into the Atlantic each second. The stream of fresh water from the river can be detected in the ocean for about a hun-

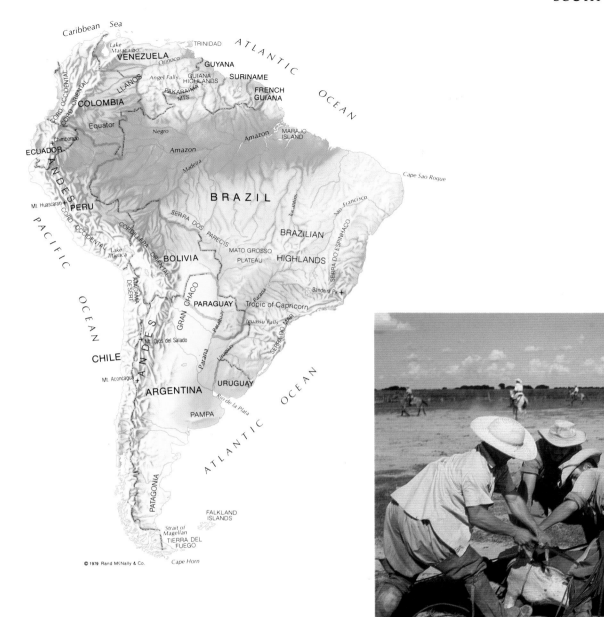

West of the Paraguay River lies the Gran Chaco, a region of dry plains with a climate harsher than that of eastern Paraguay. The nation's large cattle ranches are found here.

dred miles (160 kilometers) off the coast of South America.

The Amazon flows out of a huge plain called the Amazon River basin, an area almost as big as the United States. The equator runs through this area, so it is very warm, and it re-ceives a lot of rainfall. These factors combine to make this region the biggest tropical rain forest on earth.

A plain stretches across Paraguay and most of Argentina. It is made up of two different areas—the Gran Chaco and the Pampa. The Gran Chaco is a dry region with few trees. The Pampa receives more rain; it is a nearly treeless grassland ideal for grazing cattle and sheep. Patagonia lies near the southern tip of South America.

Animals

Nearly a fourth of all the species of animals known live in South America. But as in other parts of the world, people are hunting these animals and attempting to develop the lands the animals live on, so many creatures are in danger of becoming extinct.

The Amazon rain forests provide homes for many animals. The jaguar, a big spotted cat, prowls among the trees at night, and herds of piglike peccaries root in the underbrush. The tapir, an animal that looks like a large hog with a long nose, also lives in the forest.

The trees of the rain forest brighten with the colorful plumage of parrots, macaws, toucans, and other birds. Monkeys howl and shriek from the treetops. Sloths hang upside down from the branches and feed on leaves at night. The boa constrictor also lives in the rain forest.

In the rivers swim caimans, the alligators of South America. Schools of razor-toothed fish called piranha cruise through the water.

On the plains of South America live giant anteaters, which may be more than six feet (about two meters) long. The long-legged maned wolf live here, too.

In the Andes live llamas, vicuñas, and alpacas. Some of these animals have been tamed by people who use them like sheep or cattle. The spectacled bear lives on mountain slopes. It gets its name from the circles of yellowish fur, like eyeglass frames, around its eyes.

The mysterious Galapagos Islands lie about 600 miles (965.58 kilometers) off the coast of Ecuador. Here live rare cormorants that cannot fly, great lizardlike iguanas, and giant turtles weighing 500 pounds (226.8 kilograms). Some species have been victimized by overhunting, but the islands are now a national park and wildlife refuge.

Oil Exported

Oil Fields

Coffee Bean
Farming

Emerald Mining

Fishing

Mining

Shipping

Agricultural Area

Rubber

The Amazon

Mahogany
Logging

Brazil Nuts
Harvested

Cotton

Spanish-style
Architecture

Indians of Peru

Agricultural Area

Machu Picchu
(Inca Ruins)

Fishing in
Lake Titicaca

Soccer

Anchovy Fishing

Mining

Brasilia

Mining

Trees Tapped
for Tannin

Light Industry

Rio de Janeiro

Copper

Coffee Grown

Cattle Raising

Beef for Export

Agricultural Area

Fishing

Wheatlands

Bonito Fishing

Lumbering
and Sawmills

Sheep Herding

SOUTH AMERICA
Countries and Cities

Ancestors of Native Americans crossed a narrow bridge of land between what is now Alaska and Siberia thousands of years ago. Over the centuries, the American Indians populated all of North and South America. In the Andes Mountains, a sophisticated Native American group called the Incas thrived and created a huge empire. The lands that now make up the nations of Peru, Ecuador, and Bolivia were part of the empire. Cuzco, Peru, was its capital.

Just like North America, South America was explored and conquered by Europeans after about 1500. People from Spain, Portugal, and other European countries took over the land, some of which had been inhabited by Indians for centu-

Roads
Railroads

Barranquilla
Caracas
Port of Spain
TRINIDAD AND TOBAGO
Maracaibo
VENEZUELA
Georgetown
Paramaribo
GUYANA
Cayenne
Bogotá
SURINAME
FR. GUIANA
COLOMBIA
Equator
Belem
ECUADOR
Quito
Manaus
Guayaquil
Fortaleza
PERU
BRAZIL
Recife
Lima
Cuzco
Salvador
La Paz
BOLIVIA
Brasilia
Sucre
Belo Horizonte
Tropic of Capricorn
PARAGUAY
Antofagasta
Asuncion
Sao Paulo
Santos
Rio de Janeiro
Porto Alegre
CHILE
Cordoba
Mendoza
Rosario
URUGUAY
Valparaiso
Santiago
Montevideo
Buenos Aires
La Plata
Concepcion
ARGENTINA
Bahia Blanca

FALKLAND ISLANDS (U.K.)

Punta Arenas

© Rand McNally & Co.
X-540000-279-1-1-2

Suriname's bauxite deposits fuel the nation's mining and industry. Much of the bauxite is shipped to the United States, but Suriname's factories also process the ore into alumina and aluminum for export.

ries. Many wars were fought over the years, but the borders of many of today's South American countries have existed for over one hundred years.

South America's largest and most populated country is Brazil. More people live in Brazil than in all other South American countries combined. Brazil is also the continent's leading industrial nation. Argentina is the second-largest South American country.

Like North Americans, most South Americans speak the language of the European country that once ruled the area in which they live. For example, Brazil was once a colony of Portugal, and today most Brazilians speak Portuguese. Many other South American countries were once dominated by Spain, and Spanish is widely spoken on the continent. There are many American Indians in South America who still speak the languages of their ancestors.

South America has many important cities. The biggest of them is São Paulo, Brazil—one of the largest cities in the world. Buenos Aires, Argentina, and Rio de Janeiro, Brazil, are also in the world's top ten in population. All three cities are very modern and have a lot of industry. If you look at these three cities on the map, you see they all have something in common: they are all near the Atlantic coast. They all grew up around or very close to natural ports, or places where ships could safely land.

Inhabited before the eleventh century, Quito, Ecuador, is situated in the Andes, only fifteen miles (twenty-four kilometers) south of the equator. The city is the capital and second largest city in Ecuador.

The second largest city in Brazil and one of the most populous in the world, Rio de Janeiro is a popular tourist destination.

86

NICARAGUA

León
Managua
Bluefields

Lago de
Nicaragua

San Juan del Sur
San Juan del Norte
(Greytown)

Irazú (Vol.)
11 260

COSTA RICA

Limón

Puntarenas
Bocas del
Toro
San José
Golfo de
los Mosquitos

David
Golfo Dulce
Golfo de
Chiriquí
COIBA

PENINSULA
DE AZUERO

Colón
DE
PANAMÁ
Panamá
Golfo de
Panamá

ISTMO
PANAMA

CARIBBEAN SEA

Santa Marta
Puerto Colombia
Barranquilla
Sabanalarga
Cartagena
Calamar
Sincelejo
Sincé
Lorica
Cereté
Montería
Turbo

El Carmen
Magangué El Banco
Mompós
Plato

PTA DE GALLINAS
PENINSULA
DE GUAJIRA
Ríohacha

ARUBA
(Neth.)
Punto Fijo
PEN. DE
PARAGUANÁ

CURAÇAO
(Neth.)
Willemstad

BONAIRE
(Neth.)

ISLAS LOS
ROQUES

I. ORCHILA
LA
TORTUGA

ISLA DE
MARGARITA
La Asunción
Porlamar

Coro
Cabimas
Maracaibo
Altagracia

Puerto
Cumarebo

Puerto Cabello
Maiquetía
La Guaira

CARACAS

Cumaná
Puerto la Cruz
Barcelona

COLOMBIA

Golfo de
Venezuela

Barquisimeto
Valencia
Los Teques
Ocumare
del Tuy
La Victoria

Aragua
de Barcelona
El Tigre

VENEZUELA

Ciudad
Bolívar

PACIFIC OCEAN

ISLA DEL COCO
(Costa Rica)

ISLA DE MALPELO
(Colombia)

CABO CORRIENTES

Buenaventura
Bahía de Buenaventura

Cali
Palmira
Puerto
Tejada
Popayán

Bolívar
La Cruz

Tumaco
Barbacoas
Túquerres
Pasto
Ipiales

Esmeraldas

Equator

PINTA
MARCHENA
GENOVESA
SAN SALVADOR
SANTA CRUZ
SAN CRISTÓBAL
ISABELA

ARCHIPIELAGO
DE COLON
(GALÁPAGOS ISLANDS)
(Ecuador)

Quibdó
Urrao
Aguadas
Manizales
Pereira
Armenia
Ibagué
Espinal
Chaparral

Turbo
Ituango
Yarumal
Antioquia
Bello

MEDELLIN

Barrancabermeja
Bucaramanga
Málaga

Puerto
Wilches

San Cristóbal

Pamplona
Cúcuta

Arauca

Puerto
de Nutrias
San Fernando
de Apure

La Grita
CORD.
Barinas
Guanare
Acarigua
Calabozo

Trujillo
Valera
Mérida
Pico Bolívar
16 427

Ocaña
Socorro
Alto Ritacuva
18 022

Zipaquirá
Sogamoso
Duitama
Tunja
Miraflores
Orocué

Chiquinquirá
La Dorada
Honda
Ambalema

BOGOTÁ
Girardot
Villavicencio
Purificación
Salto de Tequendama

Neiva
Campoalegre
Garzón
Pitalito
Florencia

San Fernando
de Atabapo

Maroa

Calamar

MESA
DE YAMBI

Buga

Ibarra
Otavalo
Cayambe
Tulcán

Quito
Cotopaxi
19 347
Latacunga
Archidona

ECUADOR

Bahía de Caráquez
Manta
Portoviejo
Jipijapa
Babahoyo

Chone
Ambato
Guaranda
Banos
Chimborazo 20 702
Riobamba
Alausí

Guayaquil
Golfo de Guayaquil
Cuenca
Machala
Santa
Rosa
Loja
Azogues
Sígsig

PTA. PARIÑAS
Talara
PTA. AGUJA
Paita
Piura
Castilla

Sullana
Chulucanas

Iquitos

Leticia

Içana

Uaupés

Barcelos

São Paulo de Olivença

Tefé

PERU

AMAZONAS

SELVA

LOBOS DE TIERRA
Lambayeque
Ferreñafe
Puerto Eten

Chiclayo
Cajamarca

Pacasmayo
Puerto Chicama
Trujillo
Salaverry

Chachapoyas
Lamas
Tarapoto

Moyobamba
Yurimaguas

Cruzeiro
do Sul

Eirunepé

ACRE

Chimbote
Huaraz
Nevs
Huascarán
22 133

Huamachuco
Chepén

Tingo
María

Nudo de Pasco
15 118

Puerto Bermúdez

Cerro de Pasco
Tarma
La Oroya
Jauja

Callao
LIMA
Chorrillos

Huancayo
Huancavelica
Ayacucho

Huacho
ISLAS CHINCHAS
Huaral
Cañete
Chincha Alta
Pisco
Bahía de Pisco
PTA. CARRETAS
Ica

GRAN PAJONAL

Machu Picchu

Abancay
Cotabambas
Cusco

Puquio
Coracora
Nudo Coropuna
21 696
Volcán Misti
19 101
Arequipa
Miraflores

Ayaviri
Sicuani

Juliaca
Ayata

Ayaviri

Puno
Lago Titicaca
Nev. Illampu
21 066

Rio Branco

Cobija
Riberalta

Porto Acre

Villa
Bella

RONDÔ

Porto Velho

MASSIÇO DE
PAC

Guajará
Mirim

Puerto
Maldonado

Reyes

Trinidad

Achacachi
LA PAZ
Viacha

BOLIVIA

Corocoro
Oruro

Cochabamba
Punata
Tarata
Valle
Grande

Camaná
Mollendo

Ilo
Moquegua
Tacna

Arica

Nev.
Sajama
21 391

Corque
Colquechaca
Uncía
Huanuni

Lago de
Poopó

ALTIPLANO

Sucre
Potosí

Lagunillas
Montegudo

Sar

Iquique
Huanchaca
Uyuni
Pulacayo
San Lucas

Pisagua

PUNA DE
ATACAMA
Villazón

Villa
Monte

Tocopilla

Calama
Chuquicamata
Cerro
Licancábur
19 455

JUJUY
ARGENTINA
SALTA

Tarija

Yacuiba

Antofagasta
Mejillones
Pedro de Valdivia

Tropic of Capricorn

X-549100-26
COPYRIGHT BY
RAND M9NALLY & COMPANY
MADE IN U.S.A.

Scale 1:16,850,000, one inch to 265 miles. Sinusoidal Projection
Elevations and depressions are given in feet

Longitude West 65° of Greenwich

Cities
and
Towns

0 to 50,000
50,000 to 500,000

500,000 to 1,000,000
1,000,000 and over

Inset map: MEDELLIN / BOGOTÁ region

Scale 1:4,200,000

0 10 20 30 40 Miles
0 10 20 30 40 50 60 Kilometers

Pavarandocito
Dabeiba
Cañasgordas
Alto Musinga
12 631
Maro Jarapeto
9186
Urrao
Bebará
Neguá
Quibdó
Certeguí
Tadó
Istmina
Cerro Tamaná
13 786
El Cajon
Anserma
Andágueda
Sipí
Roldanillo
13 944
Zarzal
Truijillo
Sevilla
Tulúa
Buga
VALLE DEL CAUCA
Darién
Restrepo
Guacarí
Cerrito
Cali
Jamundí
Florida
Miranda
Puerto
Tejada
Corinto
Buenos Aires
Santander
Toribío

Tres Morros
11 155
Ituango
Yarumal
Anorí
Segovia
Remedios

ANTIOQUIA
San Andrés
Santa Rosa
Sopetrán
Cisneros
Yolombó
Amalfi

Sabanas Páramo
13 395
Antioquia
Barbosa
San Roque
Puerto Berrío

Anza
Bello
MEDELLIN
Itagüi
Envigado
Caldas
Rionegro
San Rafael
San Carlos
San Luis

CHOCÓ
Concordia
La Ceja
Fredonia
Sonsón

RISARALDA
Cerro de Parados
10 991

CALDAS
Kiosuető
Apía
Marmato
Neira
Salamina
Pensilvania
La Dorada

Santa Rosa
de Cabal
Nevado del Ruiz
17 716
Manizales
Manzanares
Fresno
Mariquita
Villeta
Zipaquirá

Pereira
Finlandia
Armero
Líbano
Honda

CUNDINAMARCA
Guasca
Gachetá

Cartago
Quimbaya
Nevado del
Tolima 17 110
Ibagué
Cajamarca
Girardot

Facatativá
Ambalema
Fontibón
Guaduas
Junín

BOGOTÁ
La Mesa
Fusagasugá
Restrepo
Quetame
Villavicencio

Armenia
QUINDÍO
Caicedonia
Pico de Chili
17 894
Rovira
Espinal

Totaicó
Fómeque
Acacías

TOLIMA
San Antonio
Ortega
Coyaima
Purificación
Prado
Guamo

Cerro
Nevado
14 961

CORDILLERA ORIENTAL

Chaparral
Ataco
Natagaima
Alpujarra
Colombia
San Martín

Pico de
Mundonuevo
13 123

Aipe
Villavieja
Baraza
Tello

META
San Juan

CORDILLERA CENTRAL
CORDILLERA OCCIDENTAL

ANDES MTS.

Nevado de Huila
18 865

HUILA
Neiva
Palermo
San Antonio

©R.M9N.

TRINIDAD AND TOBAGO
Port of Spain

CARIBBEAN SEA

CARACAS
Maracay
Valencia
CARABOBO

Scale 1:4,200,000
0 10 20 30 40 Miles
0 10 20 30 40 50 60 Kilometers

Cumaná
SUCRE
Barcelona
ANZOÁTEGUI

Georgetown
Paramaribo

GUYANA

SURINAME **FRENCH GUIANA**
Cayenne
Saint-Georges

AMAPÁ

ATLANTIC OCEAN

Equator

Belém (Pará)
São Luís (Maranhão)

Manaus (Manáos)

PARÁ

FORTALEZA (Ceará)
CEARÁ

MARANHÃO
Teresina
PIAUÍ

RIO GRANDE DO NORTE
Natal
PARAÍBA João Pessoa
Campina Grande

PERNAMBUCO
RECIFE (Pernambuco)
Olinda

BRAZIL

ALAGOAS
Maceió
SERGIPE
Aracaju

TOCANTINS

BAHIA
Feira de Santana
SALVADOR (Bahia)

MATO GROSSO
CHAPADA DE MATO GROSSO

Cuiabá

GOIÁS
D.F. **Brasília**
Goiânia

MINAS GERAIS
BELO HORIZONTE

ESPÍRITO SANTO
Vitória

MATO GROSSO DO SUL
Campo Grande

SÃO PAULO
São José do Rio Prêto
Ribeirão Prêto

RIO DE JANEIRO
RIO DE JANEIRO
Niterói
Tropic of Capricorn

PARANÁ
SÃO PAULO
Santos

PARAGUAY

GRAN CHACO

40,000 SQ MI
AREA

0 100 200
Miles

0 50 100 200 300 400 500 Miles
0 100 200 400 600 800 Kilometers

BELO HORIZONTE
MINAS GERAIS

BOLIVIA
PARAGUAY
GRAN CHACO
FORMOSA
PARANÁ
SÃO PAULO
RIO DE JANEIRO

Tocopilla
Calama
Chuquicamata
Villazón
Tupiza
Tarija
Yacuiba
Paranaíba
Itapira
São José do Rio Prêto
Barretos
Franca
Divinópolis
Ouro Prêto
S. João del Rei
Vargínha
Barbacena
Juiz de Fora
Petrópolis

Pedro de Valdivia
La Quiaca
Orán
Tartagal
Mariscal Estigarribia
Puerto Casado
Porto Murtinho
Presidente Epitácio
Assis
Tupã
Lins
Araraquara
Pôços de Caldas
Pouso Alegre
Nova Iguaçu

Mejillones
PUNA DE ATACAMA
JUJUY
Salta
CHACO
Concepción
Horqueta
Pedro Juan Caballero
Londrina
Bauru
Piracicaba
Campinas
Sorocaba
Jundiaí
Taubaté
RIO DE JANEIRO

Antofagasta
Cerro Llicancábur 19,455
Jujuy
San Pedro
Tropic of Capricorn
Concepción
Villa Hayes
Puerto Pinasco
São Paulo
Santos
Vicente

Chañaral
Cerro Azufre (Copiapó) Vol. 19,947
Salta
Metán
Presidencia Roque Sáenz Peña
Asunción
Luque
Coronel Oviedo
Villarrica
Ponta Grossa
Curitiba
Paranaguá

Caldera
Copiapó
Andalgalá
La Banda
SANTIAGO DEL ESTERO
Formosa
Pilar
Caazapá
Lapa Rio Negro
Castro
São Francisco do Sul

Huasco
Freirina
Vallenar
CATAMARCA
Tinogasta
Catamarca
Añatuya
Reconquista
Yuty
Encarnación
Posadas
MISIONES
Erechim
Passo Fundo
Lajes
Tubarão
Florianópolis

Coquimbo
La Serena
CHILECITO
La Rioja
Frías
Tostado
Vera
Goya
Curuzú Cuatiá
Uruguaiana
Alegrete
RIO GRANDE DO SUL
Caxias do Sul
São Leopoldo
PORTO ALEGRE

Tongoy
Ovalle
Illapel
SAN JUAN
San Juan
CÓRDOBA
Deán Funes
SANTA FE
La Paz
Concordia
Salto
Rivera
Livramento
Bagé
Pelotas
Rio Grande

Viña del Mar
Valparaíso
SANTIAGO
Mendoza
San Luis
Villa María
Rosario
Paraná
ENTRE RÍOS
Paysandú
URUGUAY
Concepción del Uruguay
Melo
Santa Maria

Rancagua
San Fernando
San Rafael
Río Cuarto
Venado Tuerto
Pergamino
BUENOS AIRES
Gualeguay
Gualeguaychú
Fray Bentos
Trinidad
Durazno
Treinta y Tres
Santa Vitória do Palmar

Constitución
Talca
MENDOZA
General Pico
Nueve de Julio
Chivilcoy
Avellaneda
La Plata
MONTEVIDEO
Rocha
Maldonado

Cauquenes
Linares
Parral
Santa Rosa
LA PAMPA
Carlos Casares
Bolívar
Saladillo
Las Flores
Chascomús
Dolores

Talcahuano
Concepción
Chillán
Los Ángeles
BUENOS AIRES
Guaminí
Olavarría
Azul
Tandil
Ayacucho
General Madariaga

Lebú
Angol
Victoria
Lautaro
Temuco
NEUQUÉN
Neuquén
SA. DE LA VENTANA
Coronel Suárez
Coronel Pringles
Balcarce
Loberia
Necochea
Mar del Plata

Valdivia
Corral
La Unión
Osorno
Zapala
General Roca
Choele Choel
Bahía Blanca
Coronel Dorrego
Tres Arroyos

Puerto Varas
Puerto Montt
Ancud
Castro
San Carlos de Bariloche
RÍO NEGRO
Carmen de Patagones
San Antonio Oeste
Viedma
Golfo San Matías

ISLA DE CHILOE
MESETA DE SOMUNCURÁ
PENÍNSULA VALDÉS

ARCHIPIÉLAGO DE LOS CHONOS
Gastre
Esquel
Puerto Madryn
PTA. DELGADA
Trelew
Rawson
LOMAS COLORADAS

CHUBUT
CABO DOS BAHÍAS

PENÍNSULA DE TAITAO
Puerto Aisén
Cerro San Valentín 13,314
Comodoro Rivadavia
Golfo San Jorge

CAMPANA
Cerro Chaltel/Mte. Fitzroy 10,958
Río Deseado
Puerto Deseado
PUNTA MEDANOSA
C. BLANCO

WELLINGTON
SANTA CRUZ
GRAN BAJO
San Julián

MESETA DE LAS VIZCACHAS
Bahía Grande
Puerto Santa Cruz

ARCHIPIÉLAGO MADRE DE DIOS
HANOVER
Puerto Natales
Río Gallegos

ARCHIPIÉLAGO REINA ADELAIDA
Punta Arenas
DESOLACIÓN
PEN. DE BRUNSWICK
Estrecho de Magallanes

SANTA INÉS
TIERRA DEL FUEGO
Mt. Sarmiento 8100
CORD. DARWIN
Ushuaia
Navarino
ISLA DE LOS ESTADOS

HOSTE
ISLAS DIEGO RAMÍREZ
CABO DE HORNOS (CAPE HORN)
Longitude West of Greenwich

FALKLAND IS. (ISLAS MALVINAS) (Br.) (Claimed by Argentina)
Stanley
BANCO BURDWOOD

CHILE
ARGENTINA
PACIFIC OCEAN
ATLANTIC OCEAN

40,000 SQ MI AREA
0 100 200 Miles

X-549200-26
COPYRIGHT BY RAND McNALLY & COMPANY
MADE IN U.S.A.

Scale 1:17,200,000; one inch to 270 miles. Sinusoidal Projection
Elevations and depressions are given in feet

0 50 100 200 300 400 500 Miles
0 100 200 400 600 800 Kilometers

BUENOS AIRES

Tigre
Garin
José Paz
San Fernando
RÍO DE LA PLATA
San Isidro
Olivos
Vicente López
General Sarmiento
Villa de Mayo
Bella Vista
General San Martín
Villa Ballester
Canal Punta Indio
Moreno
Merlo
Hurlingham
Morón
Caseros
Avellaneda
Sarandí
Bernal
Ituzaingó
San Justo
Libertad
González Catán
Bánfield
Lanús
Quilmes
Mariano Acosta
Lomas de Zamora
Temperley
Almirante Brown
Berazategui
Esteban Echeverría
Burzaco
Florencio Varela
Ezeiza
Longchamps
Scale 1:1,080,000
0 4 8 12 16 Kilometers

RIO DE JANEIRO

Barão de Juperanã
Avelar
Pedro do Rio
Itaipava
Paquequer Pequeno
SERRA DAS ARARAS
Vassouras
Governador Portela
Pati do Alferes
Miguel Pereira
Seio de Vênus 4625
Pedra do Sino 7605
Teresópolis
Sacra Família do Tinguá
SERRA DO COULTO
Dedo de Deus 4905
Cascatinha
Petrópolis
Guapimirim
Mendes
Paracambi
Inhomirim
Japeri
Imbariê
RIO DE JANEIRO
Cava
Magé
Queimados
Seruí
Guía de Pacobaíba
Belford Roxo
Nova Iguaçu
São João de Meriti
Duque de Caxias
Serra de Madureira 2972
Nilópolis
Pavuna
ILHA DO GOVERNADOR
São Gonçalo
Seropédica
Mesquita
São Mateus
Neves
Sete Pontes
Coelho da Rocha
Olinda
Anchieta
Realengo
Campo Grande
Pedra Branca 3360
Santa Cruz
Jacarepaguá
Pico da Tijuca 3349
Corcovado 3309
Niterói
Baía de Guanabara
Copacabana
Itambi
Itaipu
Baía de Sepetiba
PONTA DA PRAIA FUNDA
PONTA DO MARISCO
ATLANTIC OCEAN
ISLA REDONDA
Scale 1:1,080,000
0 5 10 Miles
0 4 8 12 16 Kilometers

Antarctica
The South Pole

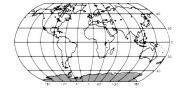

Antarctica

Fifth largest continent
•
No permanent population
•
Highest mountain: Vinson Massif,
16,864 feet (5,140.14 meters)
•
Location of South Pole
•
Location of South Magnetic Pole
•
World's lowest recorded temperature:
Vostok, -129°F (-89°C)

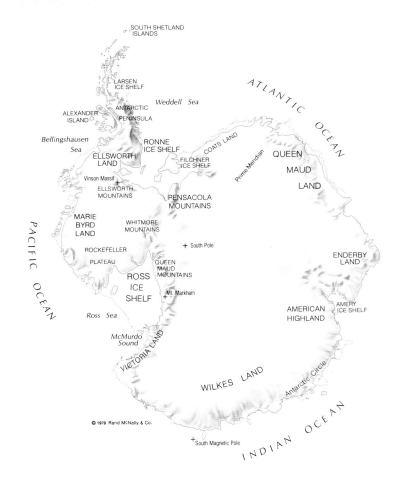

Antarctica, the coldest continent on earth, rests squarely on the South Pole. It is so cold here that a person without the right kind of clothing would freeze to death in a matter of minutes. In midwinter, which is June in the Southern Hemisphere, temperatures may drop below −100° F (−73° C).

Like some places north of the Arctic Circle, Antarctica is without sunlight for part of the year. This happens because the earth's spin axis, which runs through the North and South poles like the axle of a wheel, tilts into the plane of the planet's orbit. A visitor at the South Pole would enjoy six months of never-ending daylight during the summer— and six months of frigid, never-ending night during winter.

Even in the summer the sun gives the continent little heat. Most of Antarctica is covered with snow heaped so thick it forms a mile-high plateau at the pole.

Microscopic creatures teem in the waters around Antarctica, but large animals can be found there as well. Among these are seals, birds, and the 150-ton (135-metric-ton) blue whale.

Antarctica is the home of many penguins. Though penguins are birds, they cannot fly. Their wings are used as paddles to help them move underwater.

In 1911, explorers discovered the South Pole. Today, no one makes a permanent home on this frozen continent, but hundreds of scientists study Antarctica's unique environment.

Penguins frolic in the cold waters off the coast of Antarctica. These are adélie penguins, one of only two species that breed in Antarctica.

World Facts and Comparisons

General Information

Mean distance from the earth to the sun, 93,020,000 miles.
Mean distance from the earth to the moon, 238,857 miles.
Equatorial diameter of the earth, 7,926.38 miles.
Polar diameter of the earth, 7,899.80 miles.
Mean diameter of the earth, 7,917.52 miles.
Equatorial circumference of the earth, 24,901.46 miles.
Polar circumference of the earth, 24,855.34 miles.

Total area of the earth, 197,000,000 square miles.
Total land area of the earth (incl. inland water and Antarctica), 57,900,000 square miles.
Highest elevation on the earth's surface, Mt. Everest, Asia, 29,028 feet.
Lowest elevation on the earth's land surface, shores of the Dead Sea, Asia, 1,339 feet below sea level.
Greatest known depth of the ocean, southwest of Guam, Pacific Ocean, 35,810 feet.
Area of Africa, 11,700,000 square miles.

Area of Antarctica, 5,400,000 square miles.
Area of Asia, 17,400,000 square miles.
Area of Europe, 3,800,000 square miles.
Area of North America, 9,400,000 square miles.
Area of Oceania (incl. Australia) 3,300,000 square miles.
Area of South America, 6,900,000 square miles.
Population of the earth (est.1/1/98), 5,897,000,000.

Principal Islands and Their Areas

Island	Area (Sq.Mi.)	Island	Area (Sq.Mi.)	Island	Area (Sq.Mi.)	Island	Area (Sq.Mi.)	Island	Area (Sq.Mi.)
Baffin I., Can.	195,928	Greenland, N.A.	840,000	Java (Jawa), Indon.	51,038	Puerto Rico, N.A.	3,500	Sri Lanka, Asia	24,900
Borneo (Kalimantan), Asia	287,300	Hainan Dao, China	13,100	Luzon, Philippines	40,420	Sakhalin, Russia	29,500	Taiwan, Asia	13,900
Celebes (Sulawesi), Indon.	73,057	Hawaii, U.S.	4,034	Madagascar, Africa	227,000	Sardinia, Italy	9,301	Tasmania, Austl.	26,200
Corsica, France	3,352	Hispaniola, N.A.	29,300	Mindanao, Philippines	36,537	Sicily, Italy	9,926	Tierra del Fuego, S.A.	18,600
Crete, Greece	3,189	Hokkaidō, Japan	32,245	Newfoundland, Can.	42,031	Southampton I., Can.	15,913		
Cuba, N.A.	42,800	Honshū, Japan	89,176	New Guinea, Oceania	309,000	Spitsbergen, Norway	15,260	Vancouver I., Can.	12,079
Cyprus, Asia	3,572	Iceland, Europe	39,800						
Great Britain, U.K.	88,795	Ireland, Europe	32,600					Victoria I., Can.	83,897
		Jamaica, N.A.	4,200						

Principal Lakes, Oceans, Seas, and Their Areas

Lake/Country	Area (Sq.Mi.)	Lake/Country	Area (Sq.Mi.)	Lake/Country	Area (Sq.Mi.)	Lake/Country	Area (Sq.Mi.)	Lake/Country	Area (Sq.Mi.)
Arabian Sea	1,492,000	Caribbean Sea, N.A.–S.A.	1,063,000	Hudson Bay, Can.	475,000	Michigan, L., U.S.	22,300	Tanganyika, L., Afr.	12,350
Arctic Ocean	5,400,000	Caspian Sea, Asia–Europe	143,240	Huron, L., Can.–U.S.	23,000	North Sea, Eur.	222,000	Titicaca, Lago, Bol.–Peru	3,200
Atlantic Ocean	31,800,000	Chad, L., Cameroon–Chad–Nig.	6,300	Indian Ocean	28,900,000	Ontario, L., Can.–U.S.	7,540	Victoria, L., Ken.–Tan.–Ug.	26,820
Baltic Sea, Eur.	163,000	Erie, L., Can.–U.S.	9,910	Mediterranean Sea, Eur.–Afr.–Asia	967,000	Pacific Ocean	63,800,000		
Bering Sea, Asia–N.A.	876,000	Great Salt Lake, U.S.	1,680	Mexico, Gulf of, N.A.	596,000	Red Sea, Afr.–Asia	169,000	Yellow Sea, China–Korea	480,000
Black Sea, Eur.–Asia	178,000					Superior, L., Can.–U.S.	31,700		

Principal Mountains and Their Heights

Mountain/Country	Elev. (Ft.)	Mountain/Country	Elev. (Ft.)	Mountain/Country	Elev. (Ft.)	Mountain/Country	Elev. (Ft.)	Mountain/Country	Elev. (Ft.)
Aconcagua, Cerro, Arg.	22,831	Elgon, Mt., Kenya–Uganda	14,178	Jungfrau, Switz.	13,642	Matterhorn, Italy–Switz.	14,692	Sajama, Nevado, Bol.	21,463
Annapurna, Nepal	26,504	Etna, Mt., Italy	10,902	K2 (Godwin Austen), China–Pak.	28,250	Mauna Kea, Hi., U.S.	13,796	Shasta, Mt., Ca., U.S.	14,162
Apo, Mt., Phil.	9,692	Everest, Mt., China–Nepal	29,028	Kānchenjunga, India–Nepal	28,208	Mauna Loa, Hi., U.S.	13,680	Toubkal, Jebel, Morocco	13,665
Ararat, Turkey	16,854	Fairweather, Mt., Canada–U.S.	15,300	Kātrīnā, Jabal, Egypt	8,668	McKinley, Mt., Ak., U.S.	20,320	Triglav, Slovenia	9,393
Blanc, Mont (Monte Bianco) France–Italy	15,771	Fuji-san, Japan	12,388	Kenya, Mt., Kenya	17,058	Misti, Volcán, Peru	19,101	Vesuvio (Vesuvius), Italy	4,190
Bolívar, Pico (La Columna), Ven.	16,427	Gannett Pk., Wy., U.S.	13,785	Kilimanjaro, Tanzania	19,340	Mulhacén, Spain	11,424		
Cameroon Mtn., Cam.	13,451	Gongga Shan, China	24,790	Kommunizma, Pik, Tajikistan	24,590	Nānga Parbat, Pak.	26,650	Vinson Massif, Antarc.	16,864
Chimborazo, Ecuador	20,702	Grand Teton Mtn., Wy., U.S.	13,766	Kosciusko, Mt., Austl.	7,316	Nevis, Ben, U.K.	4,406		
Cook, Mt., New Zealand	12,349	Grossglockner, Austria	12,457	Koussi, Emi, Chad	11,204	Ólimbos, Greece	9,570	Washington, Mt., N.H., U.S.	6,288
Cristóbal Colón, Pico, Colombia	19,029	Hood, Mt., Or., U.S.	11,239	Lassen Pk., Ca., U.S.	10,457	Orizaba, Pico de, Mex.	18,406		
Dhaulāgiri, Nepal	26,810	Illimani, Nevado, Bol.	20,741	Logan, Mt., Canada	19,524	Pikes Pk., Co., U.S.	14,110	Whitney, Mt., Ca., U.S.	14,491
Elbert, Mt., Co., U.S.	14,431	Iztaccíhuatl, Mex.	17,159	Longs Pk., Co., U.S.	14,255	Popocatépetl, Volcán, Mex.	17,930		
El'brus, Russia	18,510	Jaya, Puncak, Indon.	16,503	Margherita, D.R. of the Congo–Uganda	16,763	Rainier, Mt., Wa., U.S.	14,410	Wilhelm, Mt., Pap. N. Gui.	14,793

Principal Rivers and Their Lengths

River/Continent	Length (Mi.)	River/Continent	Length (Mi.)	River/Continent	Length (Mi.)	River/Continent	Length (Mi.)	River/Continent	Length (Mi.)
Amazonas–Ucayali, S.A.	4,000	Huang (Yellow), Asia	3,395	Ohio, N.A.	981	Salween (Nu), Asia	1,750	Tocantins, S.A.	1,640
Amu Darya, Asia	1,578	Indus, Asia	1,800	Orange, Africa	1,300	São Francisco, S.A.	1,988	Ucayali, S.A.	1,220
Amur, Asia	2,744	Irrawaddy, Asia	1,300	Orinoco, S.A.	1,600	Saskatchewan–Bow, N.A.	1,205	Ural, Asia	1,509
Arkansas, N.A.	1,459	Lena, Asia	2,700	Paraguay, S.A.	1,610	Snake, N.A.	1,038	Uruguay, S.A.	1,025
Brahmaputra, Asia	1,770	Limpopo, Africa	1,100	Paraná, S.A.	2,800	St. Lawrence, N.A.	800	Volga, Europe	2,194
Colorado, N.A. (U.S.–Mex.)	1,450	Loire, Europe	625	Peace, N.A.	1,195	Sungari (Songhua), Asia	1,140	Xingú, S.A.	1,230
Columbia, N.A.	1,200	Mekong, Asia	2,600	Pechora, Europe	1,124	Syr Dar'ya, Asia	1,370	Yangtze (Chang), Asia	3,900
Congo (Zaïre), Africa	2,900	Mississippi, N.A.	2,348	Plata–Paraná, S.A.	3,030	Tarim, Asia	1,328	Yellowstone, N.A.	671
Danube, Europe	1,776	Missouri, N.A.	2,315	Red, N.A.	1,270	Tennessee, N.A.	652	Yenisey, Asia	2,543
Euphrates, Asia	1,510	Murray, Australia	1,566	Rhine, Europe	820	Tigris, Asia	1,180	Yukon, N.A.	1,770
Ganges, Asia	1,560	Negro, S.A.	1,300	Rhône, Europe	500			Zambezi, Africa	1,700
		Niger, Africa	2,600	Rio Grande, N.A.	1,885				
		Nile, Africa	4,145						

Index

Map Names and Abbreviations

This table lists the names and the abbreviations used for features on the physical-political maps. Each entry includes the feature name, the language from which it comes, and in the case of foreign names, its English translation. Abbreviations are shown for those names that are abbreviated on the maps.

Ákra (Greek): cape, *Akr.*
Cabo (Spanish, Portuguese): cape, *C.*
Cap (French): cape, *C.*
Cape (English): *C.*
Cerro (Spanish): mountain, hill
Cordillera (Spanish): mountain chain, *Cord.*
Erg (Arabic): dunes
Estrecho (Spanish): strait
Fort (English): *Ft.*
Golfo (Spanish, Italian): gulf, bay, *G.*
Gora (Russian): mountain, *G.*
Gulf (English): *G.*
Hai (Chinese): sea, gulf
Île (French): island
Ilha (Portuguese): island
Isla (Spanish) island, *I.*
Jabal (Arabic): mountain
Khrebet (Russian): mountain range
Lake (English): *L.*
Lago (Spanish, Portuguese): lake, *L.*
More (Russian): sea
Mountain(s) (English): *Mt. (Mts.)*
Mys (Russian): cape, *M.*
National (English): *Nat'l.*
Occidental (Spanish): western
Oriental (Spanish): eastern

Óros (Greek): mountain
Ozero (Russian): lake, *Oz.*
Peninsula (English): *Pen.*
Peski (Russian): desert
Plato (Russian): plateau
Point (English): *Pt.*
Pointe (French): point, *Pte.*
Poluostrov (Russian): peninsula, *P-Ov.*
Proliv (Russian): strait, *Prol.*
Punta (Spanish): point
Reservoir (English): *Res.*
Río (Spanish): river, *R.*
River (English): *R.*
Salto (Spanish, Portuguese): waterfall
Serra (Portuguese): mountain chain, *Sa.*
Shan (Chinese): mountains
Sierra (Spanish): mountain range, *Sa.*
Sound (english): *Sd.*
Vodokhranilishche (Russian): reservoir, *Vdkhr.*
Volcano (English): *Vol.*

SUMMIT

GLACIER SNO

TIMBER

ICEBERG

HORIZON

CRATER DORMANT
VOLCANO

ARM

FJORD
POINT

TIMBER

OCEAN

ATOLL

BAY

PLAIN

STRAIT

ARCHIPELAGO

TOWN

CHANNEL

DELTA

REEF SOUND

BLUFF

KNOB

WAVES

CAPE SPIT CLIFF

SANDBAR

GULF

KNOLL

GROVE

SHOAL

PENINSULA

ISTHMUS

INLET BREAKERS
BEACH

PASTURE

HEADLAND

LAGOON

RIVER BAY

PRECIPICE

SHORE LINE

LEVEE

RAILROAD

BREAKWATER

HARBOR

WHARF DOCK

CITY
AND
SEAPORT

BRIDGE

CULTIVATED LAND

ISLAND

RIVER
MOUTH

ESTUARY

PIER

DIKE

AIRPORT

ROAD

HIGHWAY

FIELD

MEADOW

PEAK

MOUNTAIN RANGE

PASS

FOOTHILLS

ACTIVE
VOLCANO

GULCH

HILL

CINDER CONE

TABLELAND

PLATEAU

VILLAGE

BRINK

VALLEY

PIEDMONT

DIVIDE

STREAM

WATERFALL

RESERVOIR

BROOK

CHASM

RAPIDS

DAM

LAKE

MARSH

TUNNEL

POWER
PLANT

CANAL

WOODS

IRRIGATED LAND

RIGHT BANK

GORGE

OASIS

LEFT BANK

LOCKS

S
L
O
P
E

R
I
D
G
E

CRAG

DUNE

MESA

POND

LEDGE

DESERT